FUNDRAISING 401

Masterclasses
in nonprofit fundraising
that would make
Peter Drucker proud

Laurence A. Pagnoni

Fundraising 401: Masterclasses in Nonprofit Fundraising that Would Make Peter Drucker Proud

Published by:

PhilanthroPress
601 Kappock Street, Suite 5G
Riverdale, NY 10463 USA

ISBN Print Book (paperback): 978-1-7346459-0-3

13 12 11 10 9 8 7 6 5 4 3 2 1

PhilanthroPress books may be purchased for educational, business, or sales promotional use. For information, please email laurence@lapafundraising.com.

About Laurence

I am grateful to you for choosing to read this book, plus I am grateful to the 26,000 or so active subscribers to my online blog, INFO (Inside News on Fundraising for Your Organization). I treasure your feedback at https://laurencepagnoni.org.

Aside from blogging, I speak to an average of twenty-five nonprofit professionals every week. I'm grateful to all of you for sharing your fundraising dilemmas/problems with me, and I hope that my response to your many questions here advances your ability to raise more revenue.

To date, I have had a thirty-five-year career in the nonprofit sector as an executive director of three nonprofit organizations and as fundraising counsel, which is my current role as chairman of LAPA Fundraising, Inc. My staff and I work with approximately twenty-five nonprofit agencies at any one time, totaling hundreds of agencies over the past twenty-five years. Using organizational development models learned both through experience and formal study, I lead a team of senior fundraisers assisting local, national, and international nonprofit agencies—organizations with annual budgets ranging from $10 million to $250 million. I have served as an executive coach contractor at Rutgers Business School's Institute for Ethical Leadership (Newark, New Jersey), where I coached groups of nonprofit executive directors, and served as an adjunct faculty at New York University's School of Professional Studies.

Giving back to the profession is important to me. I am a long-standing member of the Association of Fundraising Professionals (AFP) and have served on the AFP Planning Committee for Fundraising Day in New York City. I teach workshops on fundraising and management topics, including major campaigns, annual funds, advanced institutional fundraising, planned giving, and board development.

In addition to being a graduate of the New York University Robert F. Wagner School of Public Service, where I hold a master's in public administration, I am a graduate of the Peter F. Drucker Institute's Fellowship program—where I worked with Peter and where many of the ideas I later adapted and refined in my work in the nonprofit sector first took root.

Fundraising 401: Masterclasses in Nonprofit Fundraising that Would Make Peter Drucker Proud (New York: PhilanthroPress, 2020) is my newest book. I previously wrote *The Nonprofit Fundraising Solution: Powerful Revenue Strategies to Take You to the Next Level* (New York: AMACOM, 2014), the first fundraising book published by the American Management Association.

Do you have a team that would benefit from a dynamic, engaging speaker? If so, contact me at https://laurencepagnoni.org.

Dedication

To my little bird, Wei Ng, who, perched on my shoulder, has patiently listened to my struggle to discern these answers. Thank you.

To Peter Drucker, who helped me love the questions.

And, of course, to Michael L. Taylor, LAPA's President, who believed in my "Sancho Panza" promise.

In Gratitude

I had the good fortune of being a student and member of the Peter Drucker Institute when it was based in New York City in the 1990s. That fellowship was a seminal moment in my life and career, and listening to, meeting with, and talking with Peter elevated my life and thinking about fundraising and its integration with organizational development. It is my aim to have Peter live on in these pages.

Most particularly, my profound appreciation goes to my many nonprofit clients and dedicated staff who helped me serve them. You provided the zeitgeist for this book.

The many readers of my weekly blog also informed this book: thank you for your questions and your thoughts on my posts. Your voice is here too. Keep the questions coming, please.

A few specific shout-outs: To Stephen Nill from CharityChannel's Author Brick Road™, who guided me with a gentle hand through the final edits of this book, and whose fundraising career is second to none. Also, a note of thanks to Beth Sherouse for her careful proofreading. And to Brian Dhaniram and Tony Ross for their superior project management and graphic expertise. Particular recognition goes to my trusted colleague, Sheldon Bart, an amazing novelist and biographer in his own right, who has guided my writing process more times than I can recall.

The voices of my past teachers fill this book, the ones you probably know, such as Jim Collins, Dan Pallotta, Paul Farmer, Henri Nouwen, Dan Berrigan, S.J., and then the masters, the ones we all keep learning from, Vilfredo Pareto, Meister Eckhart, Rainer Maria Rilke, St. Thomas Aquinas, John Quincy Adams. You'll also come to meet some new guides here, Mary McBride, Donald E. Westlake, Edgar Dale, Oseola McCarty, Susan N. Dreyfus, Dr. Ralph Blair, Michael Rosen, Roger Craver, Tom Ahern, Maya Bur, and James Clear. All of these people changed my life for the better.

Thank you all.

Foreword

As a friend and colleague, Laurence invited me to read the manuscript and give him my thoughts. I was caught by a phrase in the Introduction: "a series of revelations."

That's the moment when I fell in love with this book. This is a *reasoning* book. Not just a "how to" book, helpful as those are.

Unbeknownst to me until I read the manuscript, Laurence and I share a deep, decades-long appreciation for the work of Peter F. Drucker.

I certainly didn't know about Laurence's connection with Drucker. Or the influence he had on Laurence's decades of work in the fundraising field. Laurence, in turn, didn't know that decades ago I had begun embracing (and writing about) Drucker's concept of "culture beats strategy."

And how beautifully he integrates Drucker into the book and applies Druckerian thinking! Laurence has written a rare fundraising book that integrates seemingly disparate topics in the same way a master composer weaves together the notes of a symphonic score.

Yes, Laurence, I believe that Peter (was he ever called Pete?) would be very proud!

Let me put it differently. This is a book that can help professionals explore differently and better interpret things, apply how-tos, and anticipate the next how-tos.

By taking this approach, Laurence puts the reader on the same path he followed to becoming a master fundraising professional.

He does it by revealing connections between fundraising and all parts of the organization.

Challenging some fundraising assumptions. Insisting that fundraisers learn more than fundraising tactics. Fostering critical bodies of knowledge beyond the nonprofit sector.

Here Are Some of My Favorite Topics in This Book

How to spend money well. Cutting costs is mostly not the answer. (You'll need this book to fight with your boss and board.) Diversifying your revenue is just not that important. (This one rather startled me!) Pay attention people, ROI is not just the numbers.

And here's a real wake-up call: Sustainability compared to perpetuity. (Do you know the March of Dimes story?)

All that is just the tip of the iceberg in this so-good book. So clearly articulated.

Do you know the song "My Favorite Things" from *The Sound of Music*? For me, that's what Laurence writes about here.

He reminds us to identify, talk about, and solve dilemmas. Don't call them problems. (I need that reminder regularly!) Because, yes, there is a difference.

He reminds us to ask meaningful questions. And those cage-rattling questions foster in-depth conversation and learning, which produce change.

Read and Then Keep This Book

Are you ambitious? Do you want to be the best? Do you embrace process, understanding its importance? Do you recognize that things connect and integrate, and silos are just mostly bad?

I've seen individuals and organizations learn more and understand better and successfully change–but only with this kind of *why* book. A book that challenges assumptions and explores cage-rattling questions.

Yes, this is a fundraising book. With insights on various topics, so many atypical for fundraising–yet very necessary.

Keep this book and use it as a reference source, an inspiration for a tough day, or even an entire career.

Thank you, Laurence.

—Simone P. Joyaux, ACFRE, Adv Dip, FAFP, Distinguished Fellow of the Association of Fundraising Professionals

Contents

Introduction

This is not a "how to" book. Not in the conventional sense. "How to" fundraising books have, unfortunately, flooded the market. What you'll rarely find on the bookshelves of our profession is a guide to thinking deeply about fundraising.

I hope to fill that gap.

Most of the stories, thoughts, and ideas on fundraising that follow crystallized when I served as executive director of three nonprofits, and within my twenty-five years as fundraising counsel to hundreds more.

All of them arose out of real situations.

You might consider them a series of revelations that have enabled me to deal effectively with the concrete fundraising circumstances I've had to face. They've been fundamental to helping nonprofits advance to a better next level. I've lived them and tested them over and over, and I offer them to you as a father provides his child with lasting values.

These ideas are like popcorn kernels. Remember the adage: "If you can't stand the heat, get out of the kitchen"? If you put heat to these kernels, they'll pop open with relevance for your dilemma.

That's what happened to me in the 1990s when I encountered the management ideas, teachings, writings, and manuals of Peter F. Drucker (1909-2005), the father of modern management and winner of the Presidential Medal of Freedom in 2002. I popped open! I never saw nonprofit fundraising the same way. Over the years since that encounter, I have worked with Peter's management principles in the various nonprofits with which I have been associated. The result of that work is here in this book. Ironically, I completed two drafts before realizing to what extent Peter was involved with my thinking. He has been the boots that I put on every day for all the years since meeting him. I quote him often throughout; some chapters are more influenced by him than others. You need not know anything about him to enjoy these reflections and to apply them to your own fundraising practice. I do want you to know about him, because his ideas are fresher and more relevant now than ever.

Peter was not a fundraiser. He was a management consultant with the talent and training for systems thinking. Yet, more than anyone before or after, he taught me the freshest approach to fundraising when he showed me the context for advanced revenue development. I hope to channel his spirit and do the same for you now.

Throughout the book I prefer the word *dilemma* over *problem,* because you often face situations in which a difficult choice must be made between two or more equally undesirable alternatives. That's a dilemma, not a problem. The sad fact is most fundraisers see their dilemmas as problems and therefore don't truly advance their fundraising program.

This book contains my answers to your recurring dilemmas and the choices you must make. I hope you will internalize them and integrate them into your thinking and reflection. Read these pages, but then come back to them when you're confronted with equally undesirable alternatives and you're not sure what to do.

You will find your way, just as I have.

What is
Organizational
Growth?

1

had just hung up the phone from telling my board chairwomen that, after five strong years, I resign from my post as CEO of what had become the leading HIV/AIDS service organization in Upper Manhattan and Harlem.

My hand was shaking. Tears welled. I had poured my heart into those years, the apex of the HIV/AIDS pandemic.

When I had arrived at that Harlem nonprofit, we had $54 in the bank. When I left, we had grown to a $7 million annual budget. Even more satisfying, we had a substantive growth plan to quadruple the budget over the next ten years.

True, the organization faced growing pains; it was, after all, growing. But I had done what I came to do, and now it was time to leave.

Many of us think about growth as finding answers to problems. I prefer to focus on the questions. According to Germany's master poet Rainer Maria Rilke, we should love the questions and eventually grow into the answers. I find Rilke's words liberating because, in watching hundreds of nonprofits grow over the past thirty years of fundraising, I can clearly state that there's rarely a moment when we can say, "Aha, *that's* the answer we've sought!"

Growing is hard work for individuals, and especially for organizations. I suspect it's even harder for organizations to grow well than it is for people because there're so many moving parts within an organization. Getting them to work in harmony is an art form.

Like Rilke, I've observed that nonprofit organizations grow from one set of questions or problems to a better set—if they are growing. Most nonprofits, in fact, are not growing; they're stagnant. They have recurring system-wide issues, are undercapitalized, and exert only a tepid impact on social ills. My role is to free you from that pernicious cycle.

To be sure, I do want you to grow into answers that reflect and enhance your nonprofit's character and values, and the fundraising program that matches them. I especially encourage you to love the process and the questions that arise from it as much as the answers themselves.

Hand in Hand

One answer, of which I am sure, is that organizational growth and fundraising go hand in hand. This is why many of us call fundraising "advancement" because the fundraisers' job is to advance the profile of your organization.

Thinking about the connection between organizational growth and fundraising may be new territory for you. Here's an example of the power of connecting the two. If you're in the habit of looking at the IRS forms 990 of prominent foundations, you may find that a particular funder has made a bunch of $5,000, $10,000, $15,000, $25,000 awards...then suddenly you see a grant of $100,000 or more, and you wonder, *how can I get one of those?* Well, the best and most capacious foundations look for a broad range of community impact. That kind of impact is the result of joining organizational growth and fundraising, a path to attracting more substantial awards and having better problems.

I'm going to share three foolproof ways to move your fundraising to a better set of problems, but first, allow me to set a baseline for how to think about growing both your overall organization and your fundraising program.

A Seminal Moment

"Change is what has happened. Once you recognize it, it has already occurred." Wham. This was a seminal moment in my understanding of growth. Dr. Mary McBride, with whom I studied at New York University, said it. She specializes in organizational growth. Her statement woke me up; I realized then and there that we never have the answer. Or to put it another way, we rarely recognize that yesterday's question has been answered, as today's question monopolizes our attention.

Jim Collins found his way to the same conclusion through empirical research for his book, *Good to Great.* He wrote that the companies that made the leap "had no name for their transformations." He explained:

There was no launch event, no tag line, no programmatic feel whatsoever. Some executives said that they weren't even aware that a major transformation was underway until they were well into it. It was often more obvious to them after the fact than at the time.

This is one reason why I don't consider the best CEOs to be the fire-breathing hell-raisers like GE's Jack Welch or the United Way's Bill Aramony, both active in the 1980s. These types may ratchet up the stock price with much hue and cry, or grow the endowment, but when they pull the ripcords of their golden parachutes, major organizational problems are left unresolved. The best CEOs in both the for-profit and nonprofit sectors are the ones who grapple with the minutiae of organizational problems and work them out so that long-term sustainable growth may occur.

Did Steve Jobs realize how revolutionary his ideas were and the kind of impact the Mac and iPad would have? No. His problem was making technology more accessible. Then he hit a tipping point, and Apple was doing big business and coping with new problems.

AIDS activists, myself included, at first thought we were dealing with a plague. Then researchers discovered the HIV virus. Most of society stopped "blaming the victim." We realized that we were confronted with a public health crisis involving every aspect of health care. With that understanding, we had a better set of problems.

How to Move to a Better Set of Problems

Here are my top three foolproof ways to move to a better set of problems:

1. Integration

Integrate the fundraising program with all other aspects of the organization. Fundraising should not be practiced in a silo. You don't have to be Sherlock Holmes to detect the signs of a siloed fundraising program. It occurs when the major gift officer or grant writer doesn't have fresh program data or even recent anecdotal client stories. When board members don't circulate the room at galas and talk to guests about the mission of the organization. When volunteers are not solicited for donations or asked to host gatherings for their friends and family to get them enthused about the mission.

By contrast, integration happens when an executive director realizes that the organization's fundraising program is operating in a silo and decides to break that construct. This is what has to happen when your fundraising plateaus. The CEO should understand the situation as a significant organizational problem, seek full integration between programs and revenue development, and devote attention to coordinating and harmonizing development with the other parts of the organization.

True integration includes educating, engaging, and motivating constituents, donors, and prospects. In short, integration moves people to action. It's not merely a buzzword—integration is an essential realignment of your marketing and fundraising activities.

2. Avoid Underfunding

Allocating appropriate resources to fundraising infrastructure is essential. So many fundraising efforts fail before they begin because they lack a serious budget. The principal area of underfunding is insufficient staffing. One-person development shops are over-burdened with too many things to do. A basic Fundraising 101 staff for the twenty-first century should consist of at least a development director (at, say $70,000 annual salary), a development assistant ($45,000), a database manager ($42,000), and a communications/social media manager ($42,000). Organizations that are serious about fundraising will not quibble about allocating an additional $129,000 for three specialists to support their $70,000 development director. Or, as an alternative, consider outsourcing fundraising functions to a consulting firm contracted to act as their back office. Outsourcing enables you to engage a higher level of fundraising talent.

There is no rational reason to fear the expenses of fundraising. The necessary expenses are investments to make your fundraising grow. By definition, an investment is that which gives a return, and fundraising does just that when properly structured. I've known one CEO who balked at paying $79 a month for access to sophisticated research software that surfaces relationships between trustees and stakeholders and the officers of major foundations. I've used that software to gain traction with numerous funders that don't accept unsolicited submissions. After four conversations, he finally relented, which had more to do with my persistence than the merits of the request. The software access brought in a half-million-dollar gift.

Years ago, when fax machines were de rigueur and cost $400, the board of an agency where I was executive director refused to allocate money for one for our development office. I went out and bought the machine myself. In this case, having a better set of problems meant not having to focus on getting a piece of equipment that would enable the development team to keep in closer touch with funders and raise more money. Sometimes it's that simple.

3. Upgrade External Communications

Many nonprofits are unknown even in their own neighborhoods, and people familiar with their names may know very little about what they do. More robust communications can mean mailing a letter twice a year to current and prospective contributors highlighting your mission and accomplishments. Or a compelling four-minute video instead of a twenty-page annual report.

We live in an era of intense communications with everyone everywhere vying for your attention. Upgrading external communications may not, by itself, increase your revenue stream, but it will set the stage for your fundraiser to ask for support...and if the communications are really artful and engaging, the fundraiser can ask not just for a one-year gift, but a multi-year award or a legacy gift within a donor's estate plan.

Integration, sufficient resource-allocation, upgraded communications—a trifecta of moving to a better set of problems. Numerous questions will inevitably arise in implementing these steps, but do you see what I mean about having a better set of problems?

Better Questions

Personally, I prefer a better set of problems to a rash answer. What's the allure of quick answers? A release of anxiety? A supposed shortcut through the woods of the funding world?

Peter F. Drucker thought questions were so important to get right that he wrote a book about it, *The Five Most Important Questions You Will Ever Ask About Your Organization* (Oxford: Wiley, 2008). Peter's five question are: *What is our mission? Who is our customer?*

What does the customer value? What are our results? and, finally, *What is our plan?*

You may recall the Parable of the Sower, which is most instructive for fundraising. Here, a farmer was busy casting seeds. Some fell on a paved path, where there was no soil, and they died. Some fell on rocky ground; the seeds sprouted quickly, but the plant withered because the soil was poor, and the roots couldn't extend. Some fell among thorns and were choked because they had no room to grow. But some fell on good soil and yielded a plentiful crop.

In fundraising, we need fertile soil. All the resources necessary for growth must be present for a full return on your fundraising investment. Why shortchange, isolate, or impede the arm of your organization dedicated to securing all the funds you need, plus cash or endowed reserves?

So many of us think fundraising is about getting more money. It is that, eventually, but not initially. That's why I urge you to focus on what you need to do to have a better set of problems, both within the overall organization and the fundraising program. The results you need will follow. The nonprofit that I resigned from reached a $44 million annual budget just as we had planned a decade earlier.

Always remember that organizational growth is moving from one set of problems to a better set.

2

I wish he'd grow up faster, I fumed to myself after a family coun-
seling session. My adopted teenage son had disrupted his high
school class for the third time that semester, so we were called
in for a chat with the dean.

A chart of "The Five Stages of Adolescent Development" stared me
down from where I sat in the dean's office. He saw me studying
it. "Mr. Pagnoni," he said, "that chart is there for a reason, just for
moments like this one. The stages can't be rushed." I sighed.

Development. Have you ever asked yourself why our field is called
that? I've long been curious about it, especially because so many
nonprofit executives want to rush the development process. They
want revenue faster than the process can possibly deliver, so
they're frustrated to learn that it takes time; in many instances, a
long time. The cultivation of real relationships with donors and
funders is central to higher-level fundraising. In a digital age where
personal interaction takes a back seat, the traditional fundraising

process is often judged as pokey, or worse, that we're making excuses for not performing.

By definition, a process is the nuanced, cumulative steps you take to move closer to your goal. If the goal is increasing revenue and the revenue is elsewhere, we have to build a relationship with the sources of revenue to convince them that they should share their resources with us. Fundraising has a lot in common with romantic dating. In both, the "convincing" aspect requires care and attentiveness; that's how real relationships grow. Admittedly, many donors and funders, like prospective romantic partners, want at first to keep us at a distance.

Timing is everything, both in romantic and fundraising relationships. If you pick the fruit too soon, it won't taste good; if you wait too long, you won't like the result either.

On rare occasions, the process *can* be rushed. A colleague of mine was seeking to raise money to reduce gun violence. I advised him to call a particular program officer at a leading foundation. I knew that the program officer was looking for proposals to accomplish the very thing. My friend received a reply to his query the next day. Two meetings were held, the proposal was swiftly written and revised, and a million-dollar grant was awarded covering three years. In this case, the nonprofit offered just what the foundation wanted, and the funder knew the nonprofit to be very reputable. But that's very unusual. Generally, the value alignment needs to be worked out over time.

Sometimes you'll find that a funder or donor rejects a proposal despite the nonprofit and the foundation being a good fit for one another. The proposal just didn't match their priorities and interests at that time. This tends to occur when the initial conversation between the fundraiser and the program officer isn't handled properly, meaning it's superficial. The program officer may say, "You're welcome to apply," but if the fundraiser doesn't probe deeply enough to find out if the funder is really jazzed about the proposal, a bit of hoodwinking may occur. Funders don't want to deny you the opportunity to compete, but if you're artful with them and intentional with the conversation, you can learn more and increase your chances. If your funding request is rejected, a further conversation should be held to discover what would really be up the donor's alley.

Sometimes a foundation might be enthusiastic about your program but has three years' worth of fundees already in the queue. In that case, you just have to keep showing up, in accord with its deadlines.

It might also be a matter of timely contact. As part of my year-end giving plan, I always send a tailored update letter around October 15 to select family foundations and contributors who use donor-advised funds. They may have undesignated year-end funds that need to be spent before December 31. I ask them to "think of us." That always picks up a few extra gifts.

To illuminate the process of revenue development, think of how humans move from infancy to childhood to adolescence and then become young adults and mature adults. Fundraising programs can be equally segmented.

The Developmental Stages of a Fundraising Program

The human maturation process is intricate, and many things need to be learned to progress from infancy to childhood—skills such as walking, talking, balance, coordination have to be developed.

So, too, the funding a nonprofit secures in its infancy is often different from what it receives in its maturity. (Thinking *that* over will give you more respect for the fundraising process.) The organization might launch its fundraising with a gift from a single donor or an interested foundation, but it usually can't remain dependent on their largesse unless the donor endows the project in perpetuity.

Here's how the fundraising maturation progression unfolds:

1. The first stage focuses on defining **what you're raising money for.**

This is not as straightforward as you might think. Often, nonprofit executives haven't thought deeply enough about their mission and what they're really "selling." I worked with a food bank that distributed packaged meals every week for senior citizens. Its leaders were thinking day to day. They came to me to secure more revenue so that they could provide better-quality food. They didn't realize they were doing more than feeding people—they were actually building community. The volunteers who delivered the food packages also delivered conversation and connection to the clients and helped reduce their isolation. In more than 50 percent of the transactions, the client even called the volunteer to chat. Personal relationships were being built. To successfully raise money, the agency had to see itself in a broader light, and its case statement had to reflect the bigger picture. *Yes, they were providing food and nutrition, but they were really raising funds for care and connection.*

Analyzing the quality and impact of the services that you offer is at the heart of development.

2. Stage two is **determining which revenue sources make the most sense and will be the most lucrative.**

Only after ten years of producing impressive outcomes did I bring a homeless LGBT youth shelter operated by a small church to the attention of one of New York City's oldest and most prestigious foundation funders. Had we approached this most stringent grant-maker at the outset of our fundraising engagement—before the church developed strong relationships with other funders, before its data collection was professionalized and its outcomes published, before the program won awards and earned recognition from stakeholders and the media—we wouldn't have had a chance. We waited for the right moment to submit, and our proposal was funded.

Typically, a nonprofit has to be ramped up before it can successfully apply for or seek the support that will ultimately sustain it. A community health organization I helped develop was initially supported by $2 million annually in grant money from private foundations and individual donor contributions of $200,000. I knew that government contracts would be needed to sustain the organization, but first, I had to grow the agency to the point where government contracts were attainable. Now, thirty years later, that nonprofit is a $44 million organization supported almost entirely by government contracts.

3. Organizational maturation comes later and is characterized by the agency **becoming more *itself*, more who and what it really is.**

This is the stage when your programs are aligned with the best and most lucrative revenue sources. I'm not talking about chasing money. The alignment has to be real and consistent with your nuanced programs and documented outcomes and impacts. This is also when the CEO should shine as the chief fundraiser, a topic I will discuss in detail in Chapter 16. There's a certain "period" that the CEO can put at the end of the fundraising sentence that no one else can.

As an example, a landmark Orthodox Church I spoke with needs $4 million for historic preservation. It secured one government grant and one foundation grant, in the amounts, respectively, of $390,000 and $200,000. The rest will have to come from major donors. This was a major revelation to the head prelate—a new revenue source was needed, and he had to play a leading role in cultivating and soliciting the new donors we identified. He has assimilated the news and is becoming more comfortable in his amplified role because he accepts the process as the pathway and guide to realizing his goal.

In the case of the community healthcare provider I mentioned above, organized to eradicate AIDS and related health disparities, it was crystal clear to me that we needed to secure funding from the US Centers for Disease Control and Prevention (CDC) as a major financial supporter. I kept writing and talking to the CDC for over five years. Finally, we succeeded in getting its attention and flew to Atlanta to make a successful presentation. That funding, averaging $5 million a year, shifted our agency into a higher gear.

4. A mature nonprofit will have the **full infrastructure of its development office** in place.

The necessary infrastructure for the development function includes:

◆ A clear, pithy departmental mission statement;

◆ A clear vision statement that describes the impact you seek (see Chapter 7);

◆ Operational, strategic, and long-range organizational development plans;

◆ A development program plan;

◆ A procedural manual outlining the roles and responsibilities of each member of the development staff and development committee, and the board's role in fund development;

◆ A polished organizational case for support that speaks directly to the donors, with amazing graphics and a short video to accompany it; and

◆ A gift acceptance policy, board approved.

The Virtue of Patience

The publishing industry is notoriously stingy and impatient when it comes to promoting its products. The late novelist and humorist Donald E. Westlake used to characterize the business model of book publishers as the equivalent of tossing babies into the ocean and only rescuing the ones that float. Similarly, shrewd business people well-versed in the application of investment capital to sustain business start-ups often fancifully think that a nonprofit fundraising program should pay for itself from the get-go. Fortunately, nonprofit incubators (like Blue Ridge Labs in Brooklyn) that host infant agencies with potential can be found all over the country today.

Patience is a virtue in fundraising, as it is in other parts of life. In fundraising, patience means respect for the process as it unfolds. And that means focusing on the strengths of a nonprofit and not being overwhelmed by its weaknesses. The same principle holds true with humans. You help a child grow by working with a kid's strengths. It's not at all productive to focus on what a child can't do. You help a nonprofit grow by working with the strengths of the organization. On February 7, 1990, that community healthcare agency had exactly $54 in the bank. If I had focused on that, we would have gone right down the tubes.

Unfortunately, many small nonprofits focus primarily on meeting their day-to-day expenses. Advanced fundraising must necessarily incorporate a longer-term approach.

That's why we call it *development.*

As for my adolescent son, he's three years older now, a senior, and blessedly more mature. Time helps, but so did a good school and conscious parenting. Give your nonprofit those gifts, too.

Always remember the fundraiser's work is called "development" for a reason. It's a process that cannot be rushed.

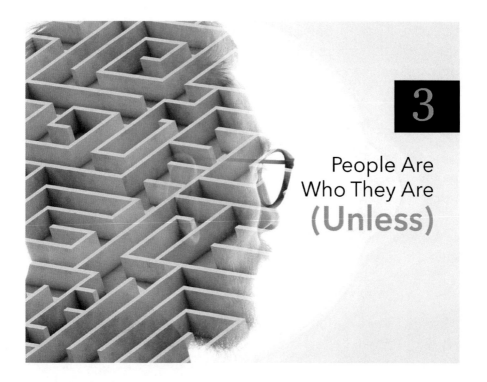

3

People Are Who They Are (Unless)

Are you like my associate, Ben? He specializes in major gift fundraising. He likes the work, and he's good at it. For a while now, he's been meeting with a recalcitrant board member who had never contributed. Does that sound like any of your board members? "You should give," Ben keeps telling the trustee. I advised Ben that enough is enough, that he should devote his time and energy to other, better prospects. "No," Ben insisted. "Let me keep at this guy."

Two years have passed. The board member still hasn't made a gift.

You deal with a potpourri of people known as executive directors, trustees, volunteers, program staff, donors, and funders. You may have found that most of them are stuck in their ways, despite whatever you may say to the contrary. The board member who isn't willing to donate will probably not turn into a crackerjack philanthropist. The individual of high net worth who only makes piddling contributions isn't likely to emerge as a major donor. *You can rely on them to be who you've known them to be!*

But please don't misconstrue this observation as pessimism. It's sobering, yes, but not meant to mitigate the amazing ability of the human spirit to transform. Social scientists, though, understand that we usually need an *intervening variable* to induce us to change.

Intervening Variables

What is an intervening variable? Suppose a major league baseball team signs a stellar pitcher with the expectation of markedly improving its won-lost record. But halfway through the season, the pitcher is injured and faces major surgery. The star player's health is the intervening variable. It's something that can unforeseeably alter the course of events.

Crisis, Choice, and Providence

My experience is that there are three types of intervening variables in human behavior you may want to look-out for—a crisis, a conscious choice, or something that can only be described as providence. I am grateful to Dr. Ralph Blair for pointing these out to me. I have observed all three of these variables in fundraising and donor relations, as well as in the conduct of executive directors and board members, both good and bad. You should have a sober understanding of these matters to allocate your limited time most lucratively.

Consider these scenarios:

Crisis: Say you're driving on a highway and get hit head-on by a truck. Your life passes before you. At the hospital, you're immediately given treatment, and you struggle to recover your health. The trauma causes you to evaluate your life and the time you have left. You've felt your mortality like never before, and the crisis presents an opportunity for you to live more fully.

Conscious Choice: Maybe you've enjoyed a few drinks each day for years, but recently you've realized that alcohol is taking over your life. Not so far gone, you're at long last beginning to understand the severe effect drink has had on your health. You decide to stop drinking and turn to others to get support for the change you seek.

Providence: You make a positive behavioral change but aren't sure why. Something bigger is calling and pushing you to change. You're inspired. Maybe one day you find that you've "had enough," and, just like that, you take action and don't look back. Perhaps you make a drastic career move, reconcile with an estranged relative, or call a spurned friend and apologize for your bad behavior. You may or may not believe in God, but the point is that something protective and larger is at work, asking you to remember the bigger picture and let go of pettiness.

Real Fundraising Examples

I have observed all three of these variables in fundraising and donor relations and in the conduct of executive directors and board members, both good and bad. Here are some concrete examples taken from my nonprofit casebook, *The Nonprofit Fundraising Solution: Powerful Revenue Strategies to Take You to the Next Level*:

Consider the nonprofit *Legendary Environment, Inc.*, a storied agency, celebrating its eightieth anniversary, whose mission is to preserve wild spaces. The board wasn't engaged in the stewardship of its dues-paying members and had not been so engaged for decades. Membership of this venerable institution was markedly declining and not being replaced, and various dimensions of fundraising were not being pursued. Fortunately, a development professional of my acquaintance had become a board member. He was experienced enough to realize that if the board continued to drift, the organization would almost certainly cease to exist. So, he acted at a biannual board meeting by frankly describing the state of the organization and its inevitable result. He called for the board to move to the next level by establishing a committee structure and listed the needed committees: strategic planning, membership, nominations, and fundraising and financial oversight. His action was the necessary intervening variable. The stunned board members, realizing that my friend was entirely correct, instituted the committee structure he strenuously recommended and outlined a schedule and process for committee meetings. It took a few sessions, but they got there.

Or consider the all-volunteer nonprofit, Antique Trains, Inc., forty-five years in operation with a $2.5 million annual budget, whose new board president analyzed its past budgets and saw that they had been the same size for more than a decade! She also saw that their thousands of members didn't usually make donations outside of paying their annual dues. She wrote up the findings and called me to see how I would address the problem. I took the results and created a revenue growth plan in accord with their ambitions to have two new buildings. Three years later, more than three million new dollars have been raised, and what had been a very flat fundraising program was now robust and growing. The board president could have done nothing, but she knew she had a choice (we always have choices) and that if she did nothing the same results would be predictable. Her analysis, followed by outside council and a revenue growth plan, was the intervening variable to produce the necessary change.

Lastly, consider the youngish nonprofit with a timely mission, Cutting-Edge Youth, Inc. The agency has been so successful that its annual budget has rapidly grown to $6.5 million over three years. The founding CEO, however, receives coaching, and his coach has shown him that he's at a dangerous period—too many responsibilities are reverting to him. He needs to delegate more and get help. Because he is open to input from the coach, he starts looking for new board members and recruits a terrific fundraising professional. Further, he hires a new major gifts officer for the development team, and that engagement has been going very well. The three of them get together often, and within a few months the trio realizes they're quite a dynamic team. Providence, for sure, but also coaching and openness to confronting the brutal facts of one's limitations. The intervening variable is the coaching and the honest assessment of one's abilities and situation.

Without an intervening variable, nothing will change for you. The leaders in the scenarios above would otherwise continue to do what they've done in the past. They would have remained on the same course...and run smack into the inevitable iceberg off the port bow.

The point of all this is you will vastly advance your fundraising program if you adapt to your staff, funders, volunteers, and board members. Gently challenge them to new behaviors when there's an emotional opening, but also plan to recruit a few new people who share your fundraising vision.

Here's a final illustrative example. I'm currently working with Hope and Heart, an advocacy organization. I know by now that the executive director tends to be scattered, indecisive, and not very well prepared. I have no expectation of turning him into General George S. Patton. Instead, I make sure to repeat myself and have frequent in-person meetings with him; that adjustment works well for getting things done.

Sound like anyone you're dealing with?

Always remember that you can rely on people to be who you've known them to be, unless there's an intervening variable.

The Fundraiser's
Product

4

As a kid in the Cub Scouts, I sold the most Christmas trees every year. I developed so many sales skills that I went on to open my own Xmas Tree stand, thanks to my dad's equity loan, and used the profits for college expenses. I loved the smell of the trees. I learned the various types with 100 percent accuracy, and I liked helping the families find the right tree for their home. I especially loved selling the "live" trees, the ones with the root structures intact. My dad said, "That kid can sell ice to Eskimos."

A lot of people aren't aware that fundraising is a sales process. You might consider it a "values-based" sales process, but it's nevertheless about pitching a product and making a sale.

Did you just cringe? I understand that many people have an adverse reaction to such a statement and, indeed, to fundraising in general. I think it's because selling in a consumer society is frequently about pitching a product the buyer doesn't necessarily want. That's irrational sales. How many ads have you seen that use attractive models and authority figures to persuade us that we've got to have a certain product? Often this type of selling goes against our notion of rationality. Rational selling instead involves pitching something the consumer actually wants. Hopefully, it's a product or service that you have fallen in love with, like my Christmas trees.

In fundraising, we start with the premise that people do want to be charitable and help their neighbors. Given that US philanthropic giving exceeded $427 billion annually in 2018, there's a lot to go around. But to successfully raise more money, you must precisely understand what it is you're selling. In practice, this is not as easy or obvious as it sounds. Peter F. Drucker taught me how to think about what I am "selling" as a fundraiser and I want to be sure you understand this right now, no matter your stage of career development. In brief, Peter believed that what you're really selling is not as obvious as the thing itself, but what's *behind* the thing. For a nonprofit, what we're selling is the impact of the service.

For example, I've found that organizations working to assist people who are homeless think they're selling services. Yes, you might be providing food, shelter, and access to health care. But more fundamentally, what you're giving people living out on the streets—people who have been ostracized, marginalized, and left to their own devices—is a shared sense of belonging. A roof over a person's head, a bed to sleep on, and food to eat are, of course, necessary for physical and mental health. *But a feeling of belonging is a more profound need, and the deeper the need you can articulate, the more money you'll raise.* Why? Because we're all human. Donors reading about your work will see themselves in that need, and they'll give more when and where they emotionally resonate.

The Context and the Case

Putting it this way usually triggers an "Aha!" moment. I can tell you why. The executive staff of most nonprofits is understandably focused on its immediate organizational needs. Time and again, I've had to elucidate the more deep-seated need for their service because they've never stopped to think about it. The CEO of Friends of Waterview Park, for instance, wants to hire more gardeners and acquire more motorized carts for them to use over the 22-acre conservancy. In the funding marketplace, "more gardeners" and "more vehicles" is not a pitch that resonates. What they're really selling is a quiet, restful, and well-maintained place for city dwellers to come and clear their heads, engage in sports, or enable their children to experience nature.

You're not forcing things down people's throats if you put money matters aside for a moment and reflect as deeply as you can on the underlying product you're bringing to market. The result of this type of reflection is the context for your fundraising.

Once you have a handle on the context, two crucial instruments help you make the sale.

First is the case statement. The case statement encapsulates your very deepest thoughts about the product you're selling. It makes the emotional argument for what you're selling, the argument that resonates with the donor's heart. That's why so much time and so much thought goes into the composition of the case statement. The case statement is not primarily about the beds or the gardeners. It's about bringing to the surface the truths that underlie your work, your vision, and your impact. The case should be a love letter addressed to the donor, not a document full of institutional blah blah. Right on the cover of the case, ask the donor the question that's behind your campaign or annual fund. In the case of an animal shelter I work with, we put on the cover the cutest picture of a kitten that we could find, one whose bulging eyes were like laser beams through the reader's heart, and right below the picture, we asked, "How can we ever say no?" That, after all, is the fundamental question to the donor: will you say yes and support us, or turn your back? Which is it?

The Data and the Details

Second is the evaluation data. Your evaluation or quality assurance person, program, department, method, or procedure provides the concrete details the fundraiser needs to sell your programs to individual and institutional funders. The outcome data explains to the donors precisely where their money is going and how it's being spent.

Here's an example that ties it all together:

Our Savior Preparatory School is a private, faith-based high school in a major northeastern city that has weathered decades of decline. The school admits only disadvantaged youth and has developed an innovative revenue stream to keep tuition low and affordable. Our Savior students work as interns at major corporations while attending classes. The corporations pay the school for the services of the interns. Experiencing the corporate milieu works wonders. Student interns are motivated to think about career choices and buckle down to their studies; college becomes a "next step" for them rather than an elusive mirage.

The school spends money on teacher salaries, desks, chairs, computers, software, and other equipment. But the context and case for Our Savior are providing a future for its students and ending the intergenerational cycle of poverty and failure.

And it has the data to substantiate its case for support. Our Savior's fundraisers know that 100 percent of its past three graduating classes have been accepted into four-year colleges and universities and that 60 percent of its alumni graduate from college. This contrasts with the 9 percent of inner-city youth that, on average, obtain college degrees. The outcome data documents the impact of the school and demonstrates the quality of the product the fundraiser brings to market.

The longer the term of your data, the better. Our Savior Prep is a relatively new institution. Hopefully, it will be around long enough to track the levels of employment its alumni eventually reach and further demonstrate its impact on the youth that pass through its doors.

Meanwhile, I can mention a third instrument for clinching the sale that would suit this nonprofit and many others.

The Tour

Site visits and tours are tremendously important sales tools for fundraisers. The tour enables the donor—the prospective buyer—to experience your agency, to kick the tires, so to speak. Tours are slam-dunks at Our Savior Prep because the students impress as high-achieving, effective young men and women. They will tell you about the positive energy of the workplace, how they were welcomed as colleagues, and came to perceive the importance of the small roles they played in the successful operation of global businesses. They will talk about their anticipated college major and career goals.

Donors introduced to a representative group of students will see the future—a positive future—taking shape before their eyes, and that's a pretty formidable form of advertising.

The case, the data, and the tour are all part of the selling the fundraiser is called upon to do, and if you train yourself to think of the process in these terms, you will find the means and the language to make your programs—*your product*—much more marketable.

What are *you* really selling beyond the obvious list of your services? Is your case for support as emotionally impactful as it needs to be, and is it a love letter to your donor? How can you convey the impact and outcome of your work in a compelling story that will inspire the donor? Will I be able to fall in love with the very smell of your Christmas tree?

Always remember that the fundraiser's "product" is your program and its documented outcomes and impact.

Planning
Is to Fundraising as Oxygen Is to People

5

Dwayne was a terrific board treasurer, trained at the storied Arthur Anderson, one of the formerly "Big Five Accounting Firms." He had heard me talk about our mission to the homeless at a Lenten service and came up afterward and said, "How can I help?" After he was vetted, he joined our board, and I sat with him weekly and talked on and on about where our fledgling nonprofit was headed. I spoke with him the day before every board meeting and every finance committee meeting. He would test out projected budgets with me, and at the end of our session I would have a solid draft budget to share with my staff—budgets that would be key to our fundraising planning. As a liberal art major, I needed this practical, technical financial assistance. Yet for as good as Dwayne was with financial forecasts and budget projections, his "planning ahead" gene was missing. I soon realized this and worked around it. Together, we created the agency's first real plans for growth and quality assurance. We became a force to reckon with.

One of the plans was a simple one-pager, a long-range plan for our growth over the next decade, which proved to be one of the most crucial documents we ever generated because it established our vision as a serious community-based healthcare provider. But also significant were subordinate three-year plans for each of our three core programs (housing, adult day care, and support services). Each of those plans contained job descriptions, timelines, management notes, and, of course, budgets and funding prospects. This "behind the scenes" work allowed us to move to the front of the line whenever we met a private foundation, a government agency, or a corporate sponsor. We could show them that we had prepared well and were aware of what it would take to succeed.

In his 1990 book *Managing the Nonprofit Organization,* written at a time when the Japanese were surpassing American industry in striking ways, Drucker advised us to start with the long-range view, then ask, *What do we do today? "Do,"* he wrote, "is the critical word," pointing out that how we interpret this word is what differentiated us from the Japanese; unlike us, the Japanese started by asking, *Where should we be ten years hence?*

Are you a natural planner, or is planning an afterthought? No matter. We all have room to grow in planning for fundraising success, especially when we ask for help and support. Not a day goes by that I don't recall with gratitude Dwayne's impact on me, and how it strengthened my planning skills. However, two pithy statements by Drucker also influenced me. One I will share with you now and the other at the end of this chapter. Peter said: *Plans are worthless, but planning is invaluable.*

What's the Point?

What is planning and what's the point of it? Is it merely a projection? The Soviets used to do fifty-year plans, and they were widely known as fanciful. Yet, the US Department of Defense has a fifty-year plan and is deadly serious about it.

Planning saves me from grievous errors—not all of them, but most of them.

Planning helps me check assumptions because what we often think is the "right way" proves to be not so. For example, when I raised funds for nonprofits perceptive about "harm reduction" —harm reduction refers to policies, programs, and practices that aim to minimize adverse health, social, and legal impacts associated with drug use, drug policies, and drug laws—it wasn't apparent to the public that providing clean needles to addicts prevented the spread of infectious disease; but the research overwhelmingly said otherwise. Planning prepared us to counter the public reaction, and our fundraising was successful.

Planning helps me seek higher (or deeper) goals, and that really makes my fundraising soar because I'm able to see beyond the raising of money to the point behind it.

Planning allows me to have a sober understanding of an organization's strengths and weaknesses so that we can present the agency in the best possible light to donors and funders, yet also share our growing pains.

Planning allows me to articulate the reasons why we urgently need funds in the first place!

These steps define fundraising planning:

1. Write down your fundraising goals.

2. Write the steps that will enable those goals to be realized.

3. Create a budget for the cost of the fundraising program.

4. Put the goals on a timeline so you can see how the big picture unfolds.

5. List the donor/funding sources.

6. Build in evaluation along the way and, at year-end. Issue a report about the results.

Here's a list of planning documents for fundraising that will benefit your efforts:

◆ A fundraising **annual calendar** to schedule dates month-by-month for your email and postal mailings.

◆ A **grants deadline** calendar that captures the date when the foundation wants you to apply, or, in the case of rolling deadlines, when you decide it's best to apply.

◆ A quarterly (or longer) **work plan** that details the major tasks of the fundraising work for that period. I divide up my work plans by each revenue source.

◆ Your organizational strategic plan should contain a detailed **revenue/development plan** within it. Most strategic plans these days cover three to five years. The overall organizational strategy is important because, from it, the right revenue sources are chosen. The revenue/development plan often has mini-plans within it, say, for the annual galas or for acquiring new donors.

◆ A **revenue report** (in Excel usually) that captures funding secured, pending, rejected, and under consideration.

◆ An **annual report card** which gives the details about the return on investment of your fundraising program that year, or for whatever period you choose to measure. Whether you make this document publicly or just share it internally should be considered.

◆ A **forecast analysis** providing a conservative estimate of revenue likely to be received. I usually update the forecast annually, or more often if that makes sense.

◆ **Donor databases** have their own built-in reports, and these are often terrific planning instruments that development staff can use to assess your donor trends.

◆ A one-page **BHAG—Big Hairy Audacious Goal**. Books have been written on why having a BHAG is so essential. In brief, fundraisers need to have a BHAG to share with a large funder who may want to invest more in your work than just enough to help meet the annual expenses. The BHAG should be a stretch goal that makes sense and is achievable even as it makes you gasp at its audacity. (This describes completely the one-pager that Dwayne and I had developed, and that was refined by our board. It was a foundational document whose vision was made manifest, and that indeed took the whole of the next ten years to achieve!)

◆ A **development office budget** showing development team staff costs plus the direct expenses you project to incur in rolling out the fundraising program

◆ **Feasibility studies**, a series of interviews with various stakeholders and potential donors to test their interest in giving to a major campaign. The interviews are often conducted without attributing who said what, and then a report is issued with recommendations about how to proceed or what steps need to be taken to get ready for the campaign.

Sharing these documents with your trustees, staff, and volunteers helps to reduce the mystery about fundraising for those people not familiar with it. Reducing the mystery will aid in obtaining buy-in from those same people, and it will deepen the culture of philanthropy at your agency.

A fundraising plan need not be a lengthy document. The *one-page plan* that I referenced above grew the agency from an annual budget of $250,000 to $7 million over three years. Every item on that page had been well-researched, and we knew our market niche.

Many fundraising plans call for diversification of revenue, which has its merits. But having many fundraising streams often requires a lot of managers, and that can be expensive and challenging to implement. The right balance needs to be struck between the number of revenue streams and the number of development staff (and, where applicable, consultants) assigned to manage them. This calculation is based on how lucrative the revenue stream is and how many knowledge workers are required to really advance each revenue source.

To be sure, planning documents are part of the path to success, but they never supplant asking for direct support in person, gathering donors to inspire them about your mission, or inviting new prospective donors to get to know you. Our work, after all, is a practitioner's art, mixed in with best practices and data about what works and what doesn't. "We will do, and then we will understand" is often the case, as opposed to making the "right" plans first and then acting. Yet planning is essential and must always be attended to.

This brings me to that second Peter F. Drucker quote I promised. Peter said: *The best way to predict the future is to create it.* That sentiment is at the heart of robust fundraising planning. That's what we're really doing when we plan ahead, and that's what gets me out of bed in the morning.

You see, we're really not making plans for the future; instead, we're focusing on what we can affect right now. Our plans only exist in the present moment. That's why I update my plans every year or right after significant new insights or donor data—or meeting people like Dwayne! Fundraising planning is focused on the work we must do today; tomorrow takes care of itself.

Planning is to fundraising what oxygen is to people—essential.

Fundraising Is
Science & Art

6

What are we *really* doing when we ask for a donation?

Ponder that question for a minute or two and envision the work your organization does. While you're doing that, let me share a life-changing memory.

I was in the back of a jeep in a muddy field in Haiti, on a mission with a group of Haitians to help build a deep water well to provide the community with clean water. Our jeep, buried halfway up its side in mud, was hopelessly stuck. But then the driver, a tall Haitian priest, Fr. Emmanuel, and the dozen Haitians broke out in song, led by Emmanuel—a song so rousing I was flooded with joy. In the face of being stuck in the mud, they were singing!

We eventually got out of that muddy spot, and I went back stateside to raise more funds for the same community. But I brought something back with me. I realized that what I do for a living is intrinsically connected with what I experienced in that faraway place. *What we're really doing when we ask others for support is giving them a chance to do something in the world, and touch and feel something they can't be there to do, touch, and feel.*

We are their emissaries.

Fundraising is a practitioner's work, where best practices are mixed with a healthy dose of creative discernment. We fundraisers apply what we know to real dilemmas and determine how to move forward with a better set of problems. We must be adaptable and innovative.

Think of a blacksmith. While there are many professions where people work with metal, the blacksmith has a broad general

---

Lest We Forget

Fundraising is a real field. Most people have a general sense of what a bookkeeper, an accountant, a human resource manager, or an attorney does. But ask them about a fundraiser, and they usually draw a blank.

There are a number of professional trade associations for fundraisers, such as the Association of Fundraising Professionals (AFP), Council for Advancement and Support of Education (CASE), Association for Healthcare Philanthropy (AHP), National Association of Charitable Gift Planners (CGP), and Grant Professionals Association (GPA). Each has codified the industry standard for ethical conduct.

Depending on jurisdiction, organizations may have to register to solicit charitable contributions and fundraising consultants may have to register as professional fundraising counsel.

We follow best practices and procedures that have been shown by research and experience to produce optimal results.

The Indiana University Lilly Family School of Philanthropy, established in 2012 and growing out of the Center on Philanthropy at Indiana University founded in 1987, is the first school in the world focused on the study and teaching of philanthropy. Today there are many institutions around the world offering degrees in philanthropy. Indeed, in recent years there has been a growth in academic research and the application of academic disciplines related to fundraising such as behavioral economics as well as neuroscience in the field of philanthropic psychology.

knowledge of how to make and repair countless things, from the most complex weapons and armor to simple pieces like nails or links of chain. The most sophisticated blacksmiths understand the chemistry behind their work, and how to produce higher grades of steel by reducing the atmosphere of the forge, thus removing oxygen and soaking more carbon into the iron.

The best fundraisers understand the chemistry behind raising significant revenue. But we're dealing with something even more complicated—human relationships.

At a Columbia University conference, I once heard Warren Buffett, the iconic financial investor, say that he "tap dances to work," and once there, he "expects to lie on his back and paint the Sistine Chapel ceiling." *That's a mixture of art and science, without a doubt.*

The Science

Fundraising campaigns have a specific cost and target a precise number of "eyeballs" at a given time. They are entirely measurable. Unlike their marketing brethren in communications—who manage branding and advertising, the results of which are decidedly less easy to quantify—fundraisers are accountable for the success or failure of each of their campaigns. We are beholden to the results, and there's nothing like accountability to place your focus squarely on the science. The science includes data, modeling, and testing:

1. **Data**. Fundraising employs several reliable metrics that shed light on how donors respond to a fundraising campaign. Essentially, these metrics fall into broad categories that record the *recency* (time elapsed since the last gift), the *frequency* (the rate of giving across time), and the total *monetary* amount for each donor.

2. **Modeling**. Specialists use RFM (recency, frequency, and monetary) metrics to predict the success of fundraising appeals to cold prospect lists and media audiences. List and data aggregators can create algorithms in their databases

that produce sophisticated models that predict how various donors will most likely respond to specific appeals. They can also insert algorithms in the appeal letter to automatically ask for increased giving: "Your last gift of record was $50. Would you consider a $75 gift at this time?"

3. **Testing**. Depending on the campaign goals, analysts and strategists use metrics to determine how donors or prospects will respond to a wide variety of variables in your presentation: the ask, story, format, cadence, etc. The tests, which adhere to the standards of the scientific method, can be designed to measure and evaluate single variables so that the techniques that produce the best response from donors can be implemented on a larger scale to improve future campaigns.

The Art

Even so, science (hard data, modeling, and testing) alone is insufficient. Donors are not numbers, not RFM analytics, not predictive models. *They are human beings.* That's why the *art* component of fundraising is so important.

Some fundraising work is routine, some requires extensive and regular reinvention, and some involves significant entrepreneurship. Knowing which revenue stream is right for your agency is key as you seek to determine which type of fundraiser and fundraising approaches are right for your agency.

Fundraisers must make judgment calls about what's best for the donor and for the organization the fundraiser represents. The two may be in sharp contrast. Is our customer the nonprofit, or the donor? The answer is BOTH! A judgment call must be made, and here is where *discernment* comes in: the ability to judge well, which involves gaining perspective, direction, and understanding. If you can understand something that's somewhat hidden or obscure—if you figure out the way forward when board, staff, and volunteers are going in different directions, for example— you're using discernment. Therefore, research and best practices are so important to our work. The data must inform our actions.

Further, fundraisers often must explain our methods, which can be exhausting. I always like to remind nonprofits that I have their best interests in mind to raise the most funds possible. You, too, would do well to help your team understand the context for the judgment calls you make.

Listening is fundamental to advanced fundraising. Listening to the interests and values of donors and funders is the magic sauce that makes a great fundraiser, and providing staff training regarding active listening techniques will go far in refining a major gift officer's skill.

I hate to say it, but I struggle with being a good listener. If I have meditated and am centered, I can listen deeply. But too often, I sacrifice that quality to the god of productivity, a bad habit that has not served me well. One time, however, I did meditate before a major-donor meeting and had the presence of mind to realize that the donor wasn't really interested in giving to the cause I was pitching. The donor was a famous businessman whose name you'd recognize. Quietly, I asked him, "This doesn't really interest you, does it?" He smiled and said, "You are perceptive. No, it does not." In return, I asked him if he would kindly say more about why the cause, teen pregnancy prevention, wasn't of interest to him. He went on for thirty minutes, and I listened attentively. I left with a $25,000 gift just because I was a good listener!

Your donor is the hero. You can tell your story through the lens of your clients by sharing how your work affects them, and you can tell your story through the lens of your institution describing its history and impact. But telling your story with the donor as the center point, as the hero, is by far the most effective method. This latter approach is the highest form of art in our field because without the donor's support we're going nowhere.

Master communicator Tom Ahern taught me most of what I know about writing donor-focused content. He says, "You put the word 'you' on the cover of the case for support. It must be in the big type because nobody reads the small type! The committee can use any language they want in the small type. If I have the big type, I can get the donor into the story—this is how you, Mr. or Ms. Donor, are changing the world. Institutions have this fancy idea of themselves. They feel uncomfortable when they're talking in a normal voice."

It's taken me a lot of time to learn how to write this way, but the effort has been well worth it. My appeal letters and cases for support raise more money for my clients than ever before. The fine art here is, as you write, to close your eyes and envision the donor. See their smile, speak their name, blink at them—make it real. This process is fundamental because writing and speaking directly to the donor in a personal and conversational tone simply produces higher financial returns, not to mention that it's more genuine and fulfilling.

Tell the story as if the donor were sitting before you over a cup of coffee. Tell them how their gift made an impact on the people the nonprofit serves, and that such a positive result would have been impossible without their support. Pretend you're writing an old-fashioned letter to a friend. Tell them why they should give you their support when so many others are making similar asks. Explain to them why your request is urgent and what impact their gift will have. Donor-focused writing is essential so that your letter needs to move the donor emotionally for them to donate.

Higher-level donations come when you strike the right balance of art and science. I start with the data (the science) because researching the donor's past giving to similar charities is a top indicator of repeat giving. In fact, most donors make, on average, eight gifts to different nonprofits each year. Then I learn all about the person called "donor" because talking thoughtfully to a donor requires that we know about who they are and what they have done in the world, and that's where the art comes in. Blending the science and the art is the magical blend.

Always remember that fundraising is a bit of science and a bit of art sprinkled with learning from past mistakes and missteps.

7 The Future **You Want**

I met Dr. Paul Farmer at a conference. Paul is one of the founders of Partners in Health. Based in Boston, it is an international healthcare organization founded in 1987 by Farmer, Ophelia Dahl, Thomas J. White, Todd McCormack, and Jim Yong Kim. They are driven by their vision "to bring the benefits of modern medical science to those most in need of them and to serve as an antidote to despair." They adopted a vision of partnership with the Haitian government at all levels, and deeply care about the Haitian people. Partners in Health inspires me. That's why I keep giving at increasing levels to them and read all their communiques. They never fail to paint a compelling and specific vision for their critical work. Working with local government officials, Paul and his impressive team are building a public health infrastructure from the bottom up—hospitals and clinics that are the people's own. They train Haitian citizens in the medical sciences so that they eventually run their own clinics. You can read this amazing story in Tracy Kidder's book, *Mountains Beyond Mountains: The Quest of Dr. Paul Farmer, a Man Who Would Cure the World.*

I was surprised to learn that the little island nation of Haiti contains *fourteen thousand* foreign charities. I haven't checked, but I'd bet they *all* have grand vision statements. That's what happens when ego drives a vision otherwise uninformed by research and data. As if poverty wasn't enough of a burden for the Haitian people to bear, they've had to endure fifty years of foreign nonprofits that produced little in the way of concrete outcomes, and in some areas, have made matters worse. Partners in Health broke out of the fifty-year folly and produced phenomenal results that spurred organizational growth and fundraising success, all because their vision was informed by hard data and solid values.

When vision and mission fail to complement one another, the results can be painful to behold. Your vision statement is the penultimate product of fundraising.

"Vision" is about the impact you plan to have on the world. It should not be confused with your mission, which is what you do to realize the vision. Nor should it be confused with your organization's Big Hairy Audacious Goal (BHAG), which I'll talk about in the next chapter. Peter Drucker said that the vision statement answers the question "Where are we heading?" by painting the picture of the goal with words.

The vision might be best thought of as the canopy under which your mission and BHAG reside. But the vision must also spark the imagination of your donors. Your vision of the future must move them in such a profound way they feel compelled to support you. And therein lies its utility in fundraising.

Some Fantastic Vision Statements

Peter Drucker said that an organization's mission should be brief and pithy enough to fit on a t-shirt. Yet regarding visions, he allowed for a tad bit more elaboration to describe your unique place in your industry, your values, and your tactics.

As much as I am personally appalled by gun violence, the National Rifle Association (NRA) hit the bull's-eye when its then-president,

Charlton Heston, said: "I'll give you my gun when you pry it from my cold dead hands." "Cold dead hands" set the dramatic vision for the NRA for the following decade.

In 1928, when Herbert Hoover ran for president, the Republican Party said that if Hoover won, there would be a "chicken in every pot and a car in every garage." Although his presidency failed to deliver on this ambitious promise, Hoover carried forty states to Governor Al Smith's eight.

Think of Winston Churchill's speech before the House of Commons in 1940, as fighting in World War II was escalating across Europe:

We shall go on to the end. We shall fight in France, we shall fight on the seas and oceans, we shall fight with growing confidence and growing strength in the air, we shall defend our Island, whatever the cost may be, we shall fight on the beaches, we shall fight on the landing grounds, we shall fight in the fields and in the streets, we shall fight in the hills; we shall never surrender.

With "never surrender," Churchill painted a picture of how the English people would survive and continue fighting, and I daresay he created the mettle for their survival. I get chills just re-reading those lines.

In brief, the best vision statements are:

◆ Inspirational

◆ Dramatic

◆ Concise

◆ Memorable

The average length of the most compelling vision statements is ten words or under. The Human Rights Campaign has a terrific vision statement: "Equality for everyone." Three words. Oxfam International's is, "A just world without poverty." Five words. The Nature Conservancy: "To leave a sustainable world for future generations." Eight words. My own company's vision statement is: "LAPA seeks to positively change the way nonprofits think about fundraising."

You can find resources to help you craft your vision statement online with a simple keyword search. But above all, it should be short and sweet.

Getting with the Times

Vision is not just about what you or others think. It should be based on research and social science. The data should support the merit and significance of your mission. Sadly, many nonprofits think they are doing good work, but their vision is from a bygone era and needs to be revitalized or abandoned. Too many nonprofit leaders believe they can't revise their organization's vision because it "was the vision of our founders." There's nothing wrong with changing an outdated vision or adapting or refining it because of changing social and cultural contexts. This is the essential role of long-range planning (planning for the next ten to twenty-five) and is critical to the success of your fundraising efforts.

I happen to know of a very large, private foundation, for example, whose mission is anachronistic. Its board members feel they can't discuss a more modern vision until the founder's granddaughter, who sits on the board, passes away. The other trustees think a change would somehow dishonor the memory of the founder. The irony, however, is that the founder was extraordinarily nimble and entrepreneurial, and would probably be disappointed to learn that the foundation was failing to evolve and change with the times.

Contrast this with the March of Dimes. The organization was founded in 1938 as the National Foundation for Infantile Paralysis and was associated with the enormously popular President Franklin D. Roosevelt, who was stricken with polio at the age of thirty-nine. Within twenty years, the charity supported research that led Jonas Salk to develop his vaccine and virtually eradicate polio. Having accomplished its original goals, the organization pivoted, adopting a new mission and vision of preventing birth defects. Revenue declined. Meanwhile, researchers began to document the increasing rate of premature births. The March of Dimes again shifted its focus, this time to pregnancy. Its new mission became decreasing the rate of premature births, and its ringing vision is now "Healthy babies, healthy moms."

Vision and Fundraising

Father Henri J.M. Nouwen (1932-1996), a theologian who taught divinity at Notre Dame, Harvard, and Yale, once said:

Fundraising is a way of announcing our vision and inviting other people into our mission... Without vision we perish, and without mission we lose our way. Vision brings together needs and resources to meet those needs. Vision gives us courage to speak when we might want to remain silent.

Without the tactics of fundraising, vision statements are just pie in the sky.

Feeling the Fire

The effect of vision on the fundraiser may be less obvious, but it's equally as important. As a fundraiser, you must do all you can not only to communicate your vision to your funders but to feel the fire of it every working day. Hopefully, your executive director will light that fire (I talk more about this in Chapter 16) but do not wait for the CEO. The fire must burn within your own heart.

Ask yourself right now: *What's new and different that I can do today that would be more lucrative for my nonprofit?* I asked myself that question not too long ago when struggling to understand the disconnect between a worthy nonprofit, its powerful vision, and its insufficient revenue flow—despite being situated in one of the wealthiest parts of the country. How could we bridge the gap between the nonprofit and the stakeholders in its community?

Pondering that gap led me to do more prospect research. By the end of that day, I managed to surface eighty-one new family foundations and donor-advised funds that my client should be approaching. I also compiled this list of steps to reach these funders and begin conversations with them, which I now share with you:

- ◆ Focus only on prospects with a significant capacity to give ($3 million in cash—not real-estate value—or above).

- ◆ Select only those with a history of giving to similar charities.

- ◆ Use the latest relationship science technology to identify connections between the nonprofit and these foundations.

- ◆ Write pithy one-page letters of introduction with just enough enticing details to secure a meeting with the prospective funders.

- ◆ Follow up on the letters with phone calls or emails to arrange a further conversation or a tour of the nonprofit.

These steps will help you actualize your vision in day-to-day fundraising. If I had not felt the fire of my client's vision, I would not have been energized to solve its dilemma or even realize that we *had* a dilemma. A deep appreciation of the organization's vision is the daily stimulus that every fundraiser needs. Without it, we're dead on arrival.

Always remember that your vision is how the future will be different once your mission succeeds.

Big Ideas Attract
Big Money

8

Marjorie is one of the most successful fundraisers I know. Thirty years in the field, she is always improving and advancing. She started as a database associate and had a few great supervisors that made sure she was exposed to all types of fundraising. She has terrific instincts about donors and has closed many major gifts.

She wrote to me to understand better why her nonprofit's donations, even its foundation awards, were usually the same size. "How can I break out of this plateau, Laurence? Worse, why aren't my donors giving repeatedly?"

I'd bet you've asked yourself the same question.

To understand this dilemma more, let's first examine why donors give at all. Among the many reasons they give is to make a difference. Not only does this make intuitive sense, but it was also documented in a U.S. Trust Study of High Net Worth Philanthropy. Conducted by U.S. Trust and Indiana University, the survey revealed that 73.5 percent of wealthy donors contribute expressly for this reason—to have an impact on the world around them. If you give donors an opportunity to have a great big impact, you'll likely get larger contributions.

Let's consider the applications of this finding:

Retention

Donor retention throughout the nonprofit sector is very low. Of first-time donors, 70 to 80 percent do not make a second gift. Take that stat in. It should horrify you. Keeping donors engaged with your mission is essential to secure repeat gifts, and there's nothing like sharing big ideas of your projected significant impact with them (and what it costs to make the impact) to pique their interest in renewing their donations. Make sense?

Years ago, Roger Craver, the editor of *The Agitator* blog, wrote: "Retention is the Holy Grail of fundraising." Thank you, Roger. In fact, retention is the holy grail of any enterprise, whether a nonprofit or the local restaurant. A for-profit business calculates the "churn rate," the rate of attrition, as the rate at which customers stop doing business with it. The heart of it is calculating the percentage of service subscribers who discontinue their subscriptions in a defined period. That same principle applies to donors.

Proportionality

Secondly, the principle of proportionality is not only embedded in national and international law, but in human nature. Donors and funders give in proportion to the goal. However high you set

---

The Fundraising Effectiveness Project

In 2006, the Association of Fundraising Professionals and the Center on Nonprofits and Philanthropy at the Urban Institute established the Fundraising Effectiveness Project to conduct research on fundraising effectiveness and help nonprofit organizations increase their fundraising results at a faster pace. See www.afpfep.org.

Sample Gift Chart

Gift Range	Gifts Required	Prospects Required	Subtotal	Cumulative Total	Cumulative Percent
$200,000	1	4	$200,000	$200,000	10%
$150,000	1	4	$150,000	$350,000	18%
$100,000	2	8	$200,000	$550,000	28%
$75,000	3	12	$225,000	$775,000	39%
$50,000	5	20	$250,000	$1,025,000	51%
$38,000	8	32	$304,000	$1,329,000	66%
$25,000	10	40	$250,000	$1,579,000	79%
$13,000	12	48	156,000	$1,735,000	87%
$5,000	12	48	$60,000	$1,795,000	90%
<$5,000	82	328	$205,000	$2,000,000	100%
Total	136	544		$2,000,000	

the goal, you are only likely to secure a major gift of 25 percent of that goal.

Trust me on this. If you're seeking to raise $100,000, a major gift will be around $25,000. If you have a goal of $1 million, however, the gift may well be a quarter of a million. There are, of course, plenty of exceptions, but generally, the greater the goal, the larger the gift you'll receive in proportion to that goal.

Oddly, giving proportionally to the goal is NEVER talked about. No donor will tell you this. No foundation will admit this. For that matter, most donors/funders aren't even aware of it. But rest assured, donors do not usually like to be the sole source of funding, and so they give proportionately to the goal.

Proportionality is also why fundraisers make gift charts. A gift chart shows how many donor prospects are needed at different giving levels. A gift chart, such as the Sample Gift Chart on the prior page, itemizes gift sizes at various ranges because donors also give in proportion to their capacity to give. A donor with an annual income of $250,000 is likely to have more discretionary funds to donate than someone with a lower income.

The total adds up to over 100 percent. This is intentional for these reasons:

◆ Costs tend to increase as a project progresses.

◆ A donor-recognition program will be needed toward the end of the drive.

◆ It is better to raise more revenue than needed so that your cash reserves are replenished.

◆ Fundraising costs should be folded into what you raise so that you are made whole in the end.

BHAG

Having a large enough goal points up the importance of the Big Hairy Audacious Goal concept, an approach introduced in *Built to Last* by James Collins and Jerry Porras. What's attractive about a big idea is the "HUH?" factor. Landing a human on the moon, the memorable BHAG of the John F. Kennedy administration, has its counterparts in the nonprofit sector. In our sector, the BHAG often consists of substantially moving the needle on an urgent social problem. For example, a Harlem-based nonprofit envisioned decreasing the incidence of HIV/AIDS in Harlem by 10 percent through a block-by-block intervention and education program. With that BHAG, the agency was able to secure a grant of $1.5 million over three years. A second example is a major cathedral that sponsored a fifteen-bed shelter, but the actual need was for seventy-five beds, a 400 percent increase. The need was shared from the pulpit one Sunday, and that very night a worshiper who had attended the service called to say he had a vacant property to donate and would also contribute $250,000 to renovate it for the required purpose. BHAGs attract more substantial gifts because the donor sees the opportunity and wants to be a part of such a large-scale change.

Bundling

What do you do, though, if you don't have a large-scale project? I suggest bundling. The bundling of your programs together as one may lead you to a BHAG. Instead of shopping three separate youth-oriented services—say, a vocational training course, a GED clinic, and a college preparatory workshop—why not bundle them together into one comprehensive youth development program? Each program may serve fifty unduplicated clients and have a $100,000 budget. But as a bundle, you can present a megaprogram serving 150 clients. Your goal is now three times larger, allowing you to turn to larger foundations or individuals of high net worth that can make larger grants.

Campaigns

Finally, there's nothing like a campaign to raise larger gifts. Campaigns are about your largest needs of all, and there are different kinds of campaigns to choose from—capital campaigns to build or renovate a structure (the most commonly thought of), cash reserve campaigns, endowment campaigns, and comprehensive campaigns which provide for the future of your organization and may comprise all the foregoing. Sadly, most nonprofits don't do campaigns, let alone multiple or repeat campaigns. They never seem to be ready. Yet, the largest grants consequently go to the nonprofits that campaign.

Indeed, the relationship between big ideas and big money is entrenched in human nature. Consider what St. Thomas Aquinas wrote in *Summa Theologica* in the fifteenth century: "We ought to give alms to one who is...in greater want, and to one who is more useful to the common weal, rather than to one...who is not in very urgent need."

A word of caution. Just because you set a lofty goal doesn't mean donors will fall out of the sky or that existing donors will give more. The fundamentals of fundraising continue to apply. You must make the case. The donors must be as excited about the goal as you are, and they must have a track record of giving to your cause. The major donors must have documented capacity to give and already be giving to charity.

But given the information overload in the times we live in, and the heightened competition for charitable gifts, if you don't have a high goal, what you'll get is low results. Go big or go home.

What's *your* big idea? The one that you have never spoken out loud. Knowing it will help you raise larger gifts and boost revenue.

Always remember that big ideas attract big money.

9

It's Harder to
Spend Money Well
than to Raise It

t's harder for a nonprofit to spend money than to raise it.

You don't believe me, do you? Hardly anyone does when I say that it's harder to spend money well than to raise it. You probably have the perception that raising money is the hardest thing to do.

"Just raise the funds for us. We know how to spend it," Daniel said. Like me, Daniel had been a consultant—a McKenzie consultant, no less! He co-chaired the finance committee of the nonprofit's board, who had just become our client.

I showed Daniel the reporting requirements for the city funding source and showed him that the city reimbursed its nonprofit vendors rather than pay in advance of the expenses being incurred. I asked, "How should we manage the vendors who require payment upon delivery and won't extend us thirty- or sixty-day terms?" Daniel hadn't ever encountered that before, even at McKenzie. Complexity. Lots of it.

Let's look at what you spend money on. The biggest cost centers in the nonprofit sector are clearly staff and facilities. Yet quality assurance and launching real innovation are also cost centers and critically important to our ability to get renewed support.

Overall, your nonprofit must be built around performance, and you must spend revenue well on those factors that drive high performance if you want to raise more money. Your staff must be supported at a measurably higher level, in more inspiring surroundings, as informed by changing needs in community and society, and reflected in quality assurances and real innovation. Allow me to explain.

Staff

Your staff is the most valuable resource you have. I used to say put your clients first, but I no longer think that's wise. Instead, I urge you to invest in your staff. To spend money well on your staff's professional development will set your agency apart.

This is especially useful in fundraising because donor perceptions about your agency's stability are a key factor in their willingness to make larger gifts. Your organization succeeds when your employees succeed, but the sad fact is that professional development within nonprofits is rare. As a result, one study, "Engaging Nonprofit Employees,"[1] documents somber engagement issues. In 2015, just 58 percent of employees were measurably engaged in their work, and a combined 12 percent were rated as either disengaged or hostile. The numbers place the nonprofit sector third from the bottom among the eighteen industries included in the study, outranking only healthcare and public administration. On average, only $1,208 is spent per year per staff person in these industries, with public schools coming in at the high end at $18,000 per year per teacher. Underfunding staff development also has dire economic consequences because staff turnover is very expensive.

---

1 "Engaging Nonprofit Employees: Industry Report. 3 Key Strategies to Retain and Engage the People Behind Your Cause." Quantum Workplace, https://www.quantumworkplace.com/engaging-nonprofit-employees

So, while I'm noting that staff costs are a big cost center, I'm also recommending that you spend more in this area because it will produce an overall greater return.

Please note that you must ensure that your employees are coordinated, trained, seasoned, and supervised so that your organization is producing the impact you promised when you asked donors for their support. Coordination requires active management, and that requires a financial investment. As it relates to fundraising, every staff member must know what the money contributed to your organization goes for and have an idea of the outcomes your organization is supposed to achieve. Few nonprofits have a staff that knows how their revenue streams work. Your mission and impact should put a gleam in the eye and a spring in the step of every staff person at work under your roof.

With this context in mind—solid professional development and good coordination—you can see that staff costs are more than just salary and benefits. And tackling staff professional development can be tricky because you must figure out which skills ought to be developed for each individual.

Facilities

Your physical plant should not just reflect well on who you are and what you do, it should convey your values. Our surroundings, both natural and engineered, have a profound effect on us. You may have read of feng shui, the ancient Chinese art of beneficial influences within our physical spaces. But did you know that Harvard's T.H. Chan School of Public Health sponsored a Healthy Buildings program? Its report bulges with evidence of the effect of facilities on human performance. For instance, poor ventilation in schools was found to be associated with student fatigue, diminished attention spans, and loss of concentration. The study also disclosed that test points dropped about six points for each ten-decibel increase in classroom noise.

The Lighthouse Guild, at 15 West 65th Street in Manhattan, coveys its organizational values immediately upon entering. Bright, natural light from oversize windows; airy, spacious walkways and waiting areas; and large-print white-on-black signage all combine to make the lobby easy to navigate. The organization, of course, assists people who are visually impaired—but you can sense its mission just by entering its lobby. When it offers donors a tour, the donors are inspired.

Supporting your staff, coordinating how they work and function together, and designing and maintaining appropriate facilities are complex tasks. That's partially why it's harder for an organization to spend money well than to raise it. You also need to know how to measure your performance along the way, which leads me to quality assurance.

Quality Assurance

Spending money on quality assurance (Q/A), something many nonprofits overlook, is often a wise choice because Q/A is concerned with measuring your program's progress, your impact, and your outcomes. Having this data is the fuel the fundraiser uses to launch the revenue engine. (Please review the discussion in Chapter 4.)

One of the highest-performing organizations I've been associated with in my thirty-two-year career spends 15 to 20 percent of its annual budget on quality assurance. It has four full-time staff members (out of 120) dedicated to this function. Each program (and each new large goal) has its own defined measurable objectives and process benchmarks, and the quality assurance and data-collection program track them closely to ensure they are being met. The staff reports they find the Q/A unit's work to be supportive and preventive; quality assurance prevents mistakes and catches small defects before they become larger ones. The terms "quality assurance" and "quality control" are used interchangeably. Whichever term you use, you, the staff, and the board must know if you're heading in the right direction and what obstacles may be getting in the way. As Peter Drucker said, "Performance is the ultimate test of any institution." What's the point of working in the nonprofit sector if you do not demonstrably have the impact you want to have on a given social dilemma?

Yet, you don't need a staff of four to track your outcomes. You can initially hire a Q/A consultant to design a unique Q/A program for you and then integrate that design into roles and responsibilities of your staff and volunteers. One all-volunteer museum that I worked with had one thousand active members and no way to track their progress. The Q/A consultant we brought in interviewed a twenty-five-person sample and created a data-collection form that each volunteer completed at the end of the shift. The forms were scanned once a week, and the data entered automatically into a database. The forms captured information such as how many tourists visited that week, what they spent money on, and what questions or complaints they had. Once a month, the consultant would have the software generate a progress report from the stats for review by the board's program committee. The reports also informed donor-update newsletters plus the museum's annual report. One donor told me, "I finally know what goes on over there." I retorted, "And now so do we!"

Innovation

A related spending complexity is innovation. High-performing nonprofits need to be acutely aware of changing conditions and prepared to seize new opportunities. Many leaders sadly prefer to continue doing what they've always done. To keep spending money on ideas that have come and gone will sooner or later lead to organizational stagnation and decline. To spend money well in life or nonprofit management means to be prescient, to be forward-looking, to redirect one's energies and focus when necessary to revitalize a career or an institution.

Caution

Over the years, I've charted the most common mistakes nonprofits make in not spending their money well, and the assumptions they typically make when they commit these mistakes. Here are the top three to be aware of:

1. I can spend money. Don't you worry about that. It's not that complex.

2. The project won't take very long.

3. Everyone will understand, believe me!

Have you heard these remarks yourself? Have you spoken them? *Spending revenue well is always complex, it always takes longer than you thought, and it never ceases to amaze me how important restating the original goals are.*

Edgar Dale, a great American educator and audio-visual expert, says that we retain 10 percent of what we read, 20 percent of what we hear, 30 percent of what we see, 50 percent of what we see and hear, 70 percent of what we discuss with others, 80 percent of what we personally experience, and 95 percent of what we teach others. This shows that learners retain more information by what they "do" as opposed to what is "heard," "read," or "observed." That means your staff and board will have to be engaged in the process of change, and this takes time.

Money Well Spent

What does it look like when your nonprofit spends money well? It means that all these factors come together and produce a high-performing organization. Compared to the challenge of achieving and sustaining such a level of performance, the task of asking for money is relatively straightforward.

Always remember that it's harder to spend money well than to raise it.

Finance and Fundraising
are not in Opposition

10

Heather, the chief financial officer, had just taken charge of a $12 million complex social service agency. As she was new to the agency, I offered her a free copy of my book, *The NonProfit Fundraising Solution,* to help her better understand the nuanced relationship between fundraising and finance. She responded, "I don't really read books like that." I smiled and offered coffee instead, which she gladly accepted. I needed to find a different way to relate to her.

Fundraising is about seizing revenue and relationship opportunities; finance is about risk management. The two seem like disparate worlds, but if you want a high-performing revenue team, these two areas must operate in tandem, and your team must respect the variances in function. Central to nonprofit finance is staying within one's budget, risk reduction, safety, and appropriate accounting controls. In contrast, nonprofit fundraising seeks to grasp opportunities, explore donor/funder interests, and deal with uncertainties like funders changing their priorities, donors failing to honor their pledge, or campaigns losing momentum. The two functions are seemingly at odds and often make their respective staff nervous.

Eye to Eye

I've witnessed these organizational tensions for more than twenty-five years, so my pearls of wisdom are borne from up-close experiences. But the facts speak for themselves:

According to *The NonProfit Times*, "More than half (56 percent) of surveyed fundraising professionals describe their relationship with co-workers in finance as somewhat or not at all collaborative, as compared to 45 percent of finance professionals who answered that way."[2]

Further, "Differences might rear their head technologically, generationally and in communications." The 2015 survey of more than 1400 professionals in both fields also revealed that when asked what they wish the other side knew, fundraisers listed, "You have to spend money to make money" and "We need room for flexibility." Finance personnel said, "My job is complex and time-consuming" and wished for a "Better understanding of basic accounting" from fundraisers.[3] Both departments listed "Differing priorities" as one of their top challenges in working with the other side.

On the other hand, I'm always worried when the chief financial officer is a member of the development committee. When I was a nonprofit CEO, I made sure that it occurred infrequently. I'm not saying that keeping the finance and development staff apart is a "best practice," but it has become my practice because of the fundamental differences in training needs for the respective staff members and how each views the organization from their own vantage point.

---

2 "Finance and Fundraising Equals Water and Oil" by Andy Segedin, February 17, 2016.
3 For a copy of the Nonprofit Finance Study 2018, see www.abila.com.

Should finance managers leave fundraising alone? Should fundraisers leave finance alone? Total separation is unlikely and can be troublesome. The fact is that the finance office must manage and account for the funds that are brought in, and the fundraisers have to verify and report that the funds were well spent, so total separation isn't wise. Maybe appropriate arm's-length respect is what we're after? On the more positive side, your nonprofit organization can create a strategic advantage by developing a strong relationship between your fundraising and finance arms.

Three Best Practices

I suggest three best practices for navigating these issues:

1. Reviews: The CEO or the deputy director should bring the chief financial officer (CFO) and the chief development officer together two or three times a year for a high-level private review of the revenue and expense numbers. Each party should submit their analysis in writing beforehand and present the data at the start of the meeting.

2. Software: Most finance and/or donor management software has integration features built in so that the finance and fundraising staff have access to the required numbers. Even so, most nonprofits don't use that feature. You may want to reconsider. For example, QuickBooks integrates with almost all fundraising software, yet that feature is rarely used.

3. Pledge: It's essential to garner a personal pledge from the heads of the finance and fundraising divisions to avoid the big mistake of disagreeing publicly over the budget. It's the CEO's job to make sure this firewall is in place. If not, the board and the chief executive will be less likely to back the ideas of either branch.

When your fundraising and finance staff work well together, your nonprofit can grow and flourish. Lack of communication between these two functions can lead to significant consequences. After years of on-the-ground experience as a nonprofit fundraiser and

private sector executive, I'm convinced that these two departments can deeply benefit each other. In fact, that collaboration
can ultimately change the dynamic and influence your nonprofit's
future direction.

Maybe you're wondering how I dealt with Heather? I did find a
way in. Heather could have been a significant obstruction; she had
that kind of personality. But with the help of one of my fundraising
colleagues, we approached her as a resource essential to securing
more revenue. We asked her what financial burden worried her
the most. She told us that one of the agency's homeless programs
was burning through precious general support funds. We asked
her to show us the numbers, and we also interviewed the program
director to learn her perspective. Then we did research and found
that their current state grant could be expanded from $140,000 to
$640,000! When the deadline came up again, thankfully just a few
months later, we handled the reapplication and were successful in
securing the higher amount. After that, Heather became an ally.

Finally, take comfort in the sociological evidence. Sufi philoso-
pher Idries Shah reminds us, "the people who make the best
friends are not those who are attracted to one another, or to each
other's ideas, at first. On the contrary, it has been shown that the
person who opposes you is likely to become a firmer friend than
the one who becomes your friend immediately." This is the power
of a team when it becomes more than the sum of its parts.

When Heather left that CFO position, I helped her find her next
position. In the interview, she told me she boasted that she knew a
whole lot more about fundraising than many other CFOs. She got
the job with a 30 percent pay increase.

Always remember that finance and fundraising are not in
opposition.

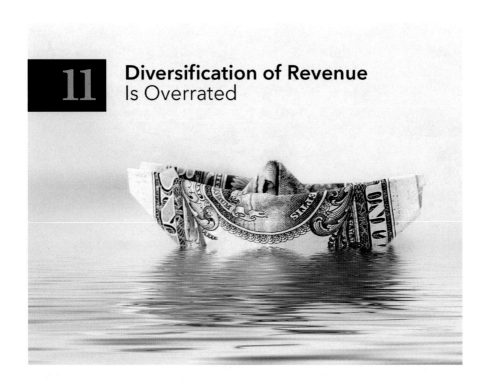

11 Diversification of Revenue
Is Overrated

few years ago, I was hired by a first-time executive director to increase revenue for a recreation and conservation park, which I'll call High Ridge Park. High Ridge was operating on a mix of private grants, individual donations, and one large annual event. I suggested exploring government grants, but she disagreed.

Undaunted, my team did some research and discovered a state environmental department that offered, through a competitive grant process, four funding opportunities that fit High Ridge perfectly and came in at around $650,000 each. I called the department for an exploratory conversation. "I'm from High Ridge Park," I said when I reached the appropriate program officer. Her reply: "What took you so long to get in touch with us?"

I projected that if High Ridge were to shift its energy to government grants and major gifts, within three years it would double its budget. What we're looking for in diversification (or, as we'll explore, un-diversifying) is a revenue source that can grow and unfold more opportunities as you learn more about it.

Be aware, too, that while wading into or leaving a revenue stream might seem difficult or easy, you must conduct sufficient research before taking the leap. My pursuit of funds from the Centers for Disease Control and Prevention (CDC) for a minority healthcare nonprofit, for example, took five years before I was able to secure a contract for that social service agency. But, as I determined well beforehand, the CDC funding was so significant it justified my tenaciousness.

Let's take a closer look at the ingrained dogma of diversity of funding. I was trained to believe that having multiple revenue streams was prudent because if one failed, you had a back-up. Sound familiar? The nonprofits I've worked for typically had five or six revenue streams: an annual gala, a smallish list of individual donors, a few government contracts, a nice group of private foundations, and program member fees, for example. Does that sound like yours?

Something I've discovered, though, is that it takes a lot of work to manage multiple revenue streams—more work than you might imagine. Each stream has its own nuances and management requirements, which can become terribly complicated to manage.

Research Says...

Having just raised over $200 million entirely from a handful of large private foundations for a national journalism nonprofit, I started to break free from this constricting idea of diversification when I read a research paper, "How Nonprofits Get Really Big." In a surprising study challenging the norm, William Foster and Gail Fine of the Bridgespan Group discovered that, "Since 1970, more than 200,000 nonprofits have opened in the US, but only 144 of them have reached $50 million in annual revenue."[4] Most of these elite nonprofits succeeded by raising "the bulk of their money from a single type of funder such as corporations or government—and not, as conventional wisdom would recommend, by going after diverse sources of funding." In their paper, Foster and Fine identified:

---

4 *Stanford Social Innovation Review,* Spring 2007.

three important practices common among nonprofits that suc-
ceeded in building large-scale funding models: (1) They devel-
oped funding in one concentrated source rather than across
diverse sources; (2) they found a funding source that was a
natural match to their mission and beneficiaries; and (3) they
built a professional organization and structure around this
funding model.

Bridgespan "obtained solid financial data for 110 of the 144 high-growth nonprofits" Foster and Fine identified. "Of the 110," the report continued, "roughly 90 percent had a single dominant source of funding—such as government, individual, or corporate gifts. And, on average, that dominant funding source accounted for just over 90 percent of the organization's total funding." The researchers interviewed twenty-one leaders of these nonprofits and found a stunning example of what we discussed in Chapter 6:

Only a few...knew from the start where they would find their most promising funding sources. Often, they were uncertain about which source was most promising. But as these organizations pursued their growth, they realized which sources of funding seemed most promising and were willing to concentrate their efforts on that source, recruiting people and creating organizations that could best pursue that funding source.

Contradicting the Norm

This is a radically unsung approach to fundraising. Ironically, smaller nonprofits tend to pursue more diversification than larger ones—an awkward situation because small organizations have fewer staff to manage these streams. Small and midsized nonprofits understandably need a reasonable amount of fiscal back-up, and diversification of your revenue streams is imperative even when you have a dominant source of revenue—and especially as you see to grow your budget.

Even so, pursuing diversification for too long can have undesirable consequences. One is that you'll likely experience a serious funding plateau, which is why, in part, 70 percent of US nonprofits *don't* get big. Another consequence is that you'll eventually need to end or downplay a revenue stream, which occurs when you find a more significant funder whose ROI would be substantially higher than your current one.

Both situations result from not evaluating and challenging your fundraising performance and from not wanting to do things differently. These problems are understandable; nonprofit executives are often overwhelmed. "I have all I can do to keep things going as they are," they'll tell me. That's essentially the problem when it comes to diversification.

The question is, *should you go deeper into any one revenue source, and how much time should you allocate to it?* I suggest that to be properly prepared to diversify or deepen your revenue streams, the following guidelines will serve you well.

Control Costs

Realize that revenue diversification is not just about *growing* revenues. It's also about controlling operational and fundraising costs. It costs money to diversify. My staff tires of hearing me say, "The easiest way to raise revenue is not to spend it." Frugality has its place within every nonprofit. Here are a few examples of how to control costs:

◆ Using nationwide published salary surveys can prevent you from overpaying for a staff person. Unfortunately, many of my clients don't use them. Salary surveys can help you forecast the right budget for a new initiative so that you're raising an adequate amount of funds from a new stream. Using salary surveys can also help you retain quality development staff and reduce staff turnover, which can be wildly expensive. They can even help you avoid overpaying staff in the eyes of the Internal Revenue Service since doing so can result in intermediate sanctions (aka penalties).

◆ Controlling costs also means conducting a quarterly review of your organizational budget to see how close you are to what you had initially budgeted for development and other functions. Regular budget modifications allow you to capture changes and adjust the budget. I consider these financial reports essential to monitoring the revenue blend closely and carefully.

◆ Gather competitive bids from multiple vendors. You'll learn a lot in the process. It's not just about picking the lowest vendor, either; sometimes, the highest vendor includes services that will make your fundraising really perform, so stay open to the process.

◆ Of course, too much frugality is another problem. In Chapter 13, I will talk more about cutting costs but with an eye to the peril of underfunding the development function.

Develop Curiosity

Saying, "Tell me more." is one of my favorite active listening phrases, and it's so important when thinking about revenue diversification. Showing curiosity and then listening deeply may open new avenues or new financial management approaches. For example, I recently found out from a certified public account a new, legal way to charge temporary help expenses that reduced fundraising and other organizational expenses. In another instance, I heard a high-level healthcare consultant mention a nuance in using a state license. When I called him the next day, he graciously explained more about an often-overlooked billing code. I asked him to meet with my client, and the knowledge he shared will allow my client to bill an additional $760,000 annually to the state for much-needed respite care for the developmentally disabled. Curiosity leads to creative solutions for enhanced revenue.

Set Planning Time

I urge you to set aside quiet planning time just for yourself, preferably off-site. My mentor Peter F. Drucker took time away every August to examine his past year and assess what worked, what he should stop doing, and what tasks he wanted to put more time into.

He told me it was the most important meeting he took all year—a meeting with himself. He made substantial decisions on these occasions and realized that how he spent his time was his greatest asset. In my own time away, I dedicate time to research the latest data on various revenue streams. This is how I realized many years back how lucrative planned giving was as a revenue stream and why those nonprofits that had individual major donors were primed for adding planned giving to their fundraising strategy.

Restrictions and/or Changing Policies

Staying current with new changes and restrictions required by your funding sources is very important when you diversify revenue, and that task should never be overlooked. You don't want to be surprised by new regulations or have to pay penalties—or worse, must return the funds—for non-compliance. Between 2014 and 2016, the state of New York filed numerous lawsuits against mostly reputable nonprofits, asking them to return millions in contracted revenue because the nonprofits didn't follow their new regulations and overbilled the state. It was awful. I found two nonprofits that didn't have this problem and asked them what they knew that most of the others did not. The answer was that they paid a lobbying firm to monitor the state funding streams because they were so dependent on these funds that they couldn't risk jeopardizing them. They built the expense into the cost of doing business, and it saved them from potential disaster.

Timing

Knowing the right time to grow your revenue program is critical. You have to be ready, and that means having solid knowledge about your potential revenue source, a plan for pursuing it, and insight as to your ability to compete for the award. Moreover, the revenue source has to make sense within your nonprofit's field of service.

Recently, an inexperienced nonprofit CEO told me that she wanted to diversify to a new source of revenue to get away from the $34 million in government funds the agency was relying on. Another source as lucrative as the one she had? My ears perked up. She was making a very tall order. I pressed her for details, and what I heard was frustration about navigating the regulations on this reliable, albeit bureaucratic, source of revenue. Per the conventional wisdom, I always want nonprofits to have a strong second source of revenue, which her agency had in the form of individual donors and a generous board of directors. But abandon the substantial existing secured contracts? I think not! I set up a meeting between her and the government funder so that she could be properly oriented, and she now has a greater understanding of the regulations and appreciation for just how lucrative that state funding is. It wasn't time to switch revenue sources, but it *was* time to learn more about the current dominant source.

To Diversify or Not to Diversify...

It's been more than a decade since Foster and Fine published their landmark study, and the nonprofit sector still hasn't caught up with their findings. True, what works today may fall short tomorrow, so it's essential to understand your revenue options and formulate specific plans for hedging your developmental bets. But a clear conception of the costs of secondary and tertiary streams must guide your assessment of this dilemma.

Making the decision to quit an existing source of funds is not easy. But the unintended consequence of continuing a revenue source with limited possibilities is missing an opportunity. And that unintended consequence needs to be brought into the light of day in the world of nonprofit fundraising.

Always remember that diversification of revenue is not always the best route to a more stable revenue stream.

A Nonprofit Has Multiple Bottom Lines

12

ominic, the chief operating officer, was annoyed with me. While negotiating a contract with my company, he said, "Bottom line me." He was asking me to leave out the details of an explanation and skip to what he judged was the important part. "There are multiple bottom lines to your dilemma," I suggested, "not just one." He grimaced.

I hope you won't also be annoyed when I explain this essential reality: *The bottom line is that a single determining factor, profit, or loss, is not sufficient to explain the success or failure of a complex organization, be it for-profit or nonprofit. It never has been.* There are numerous factors your nonprofit must consider in assessing its success, and each one has its own unique determinants.

The line at the bottom of a financial report shows the net revenue or loss. This is the organization's "bottom line," which is widely considered the determining measure of success or failure. But that's not always the case.

In the early 1980s, cooperative work theorists argued that orga-nizations should measure and report on three factors—financial performance, social wealth creation, and environmental respon-sibility. In the 1990s, the phrase "triple bottom line" (TBL) became popular as an accounting framework. An article in the *Indiana Business Review* refers to TBL as "the three Ps: people, planet, and profits."[5] Some organizations have adopted TBL to evaluate their real performance and impact.

Five More

I like the TBL construct, and in its spirit, here are five additional bottom lines that you and your nonprofit are juggling. Ignore them at your peril. Understanding them, however, will help you think more deeply about fundraising.

Staff

Nonprofits usually focus on their clients first and strive to show how their services improve their clients' lives. That makes sense. Yet many of us who have directed nonprofits know that for clients to be served well, the staff must be supported, trained, and focused on your mission. The former CEO of HCL Technologies, Vineet Nayar, practiced this approach and wrote about it in his landmark book, *Employees First, Customers Second: Turning Conventional Management Upside Down*. Recommending that we prioritize employees over customers, Nayar made the connection between valuing staff development and realizing higher brand loyalty and staff retention.

The bottom line in this instance is that we must do a better job with staff training and professional development. While staff turn-over is a significant problem in the nonprofit sector, and the cost savings of retaining your staff (as opposed to rehiring and retrain-ing new staff) are well-documented, nonprofits are notorious for dedicating hardly any resources toward staff development. Tech

---

5 "The Triple Bottom Line: What Is It and How Does It Work?" by Timothy F. Slaper, PhD and Tanya J. Hall, Volume 86, No. 1, Spring 2011.

Impact, a nonprofit organization itself, took a closer look at the causes of nonprofit turnover and, in 2016, published, "*15 Reasons Why Nonprofit Employees Quit.*"[6] It found that employees generally leave nonprofits because they're underpaid, they lack upward mobility, and their workloads are excessive.

A colleague, Maya Bur, suggests[7]:

Allowing employees more opportunities to move up in the workplace is a good starting point. One benefit of hiring internally is that employees will see more career possibility within your organization. Upward mobility is a strong motivator in the workplace. It also means employees filling new positions will already have vast background knowledge on the organization and on job function. It's also important to combat burnout in any way possible. One way to do this is to allow flexible hours. Showing that your organization values employees and their efforts will improve retention, productivity, and morale.

When development staff leave, they take valuable knowledge of your fundraising program with them, and their replacements have to start from scratch. The amount of revenue you secure will surely take a hit. This is why staff retention is a bottom-line factor in fundraising success.

Volunteers

Eighty-nine percent of high-net-worth individuals volunteer with nonprofits. *89 percent.* Now that's a stat to meditate on. It means you must include an option for volunteering with your agency in all your donor correspondence because volunteering is a key part of donor engagement. I realize that a lot of agencies struggle with insufficient capacity to manage volunteers, so you should keep it simple. Consider asking for volunteer help for your board committees, or that special task force your executive director requested. Don't you need an extra hand with your gala coordination? Take

6 https://blog.techimpact.org/infographic-why-nonprofits-employees-quit
7 "Why the High Employee-Turnover Rate?" https://www.nonprofitpro.com/article/43895/

time to think about the many simple ways donors can get involved, then offer them options.

Why focus on volunteers? Because volunteering and increased individual giving go hand in hand! The nonprofit watchdog group, Independent Sector, now calculates a volunteer hour to be worth $24.14 and has determined that the monetary value increased nationally by 2.5 percent in 2017, with nearly 63 million Americans volunteering about eight billion hours of time, talent, and effort. These figures, estimated from data collected in 2016, demonstrate the incredible contributions volunteers make to our organizations and communities. They're part of your bottom line, whether you notice.

Board

Your board of directors can give your organization more of a legacy gift than any staff person. Why? Because the staff's work is focused on day-to-day operations, while the board, on the other hand, can contemplate a ten- to fifty-year view. Of course, they'll need the right guidance, coaching, and support. Be that as it may, you, too, can have a high-functioning board, and I consider that a bottom-line goal to embrace.

I haven't always felt that way, though. In fact, after my first two executive directorships, I seriously questioned the viability of the board's role and governance model. I was so troubled about it that I enrolled in graduate studies at New York University's Wagner School of Public Service, so I could sort out that experience. I came to realize that the executive director must play a vital role in developing the board, and I had not sufficiently supported the two boards with whom I had previously worked.

I failed to realize that the demand for board members exceeds the supply of experienced, knowledgeable trustees who understand their role. As it turns out, this is a widespread issue among non-profit boards. A 2015 survey conducted by Stanford researchers, for example, interviewed 924 trustees and found that many of them were ill-prepared for their managerial responsibilities.[8] I met the letter of the law in scheduling meetings, but I did not help my trustees excel. I had not seen the board as a significant part of the bottom line, which didn't promote organizational stability after I left. I encourage you to learn faster than I did!

Serving Your Clients

Impact evaluation and outcome measurement are critical tools to ensure that your agency is working for your clients and achieving its mission. Although the nonprofit world has made progress in giving due attention to this bottom line over the past thirty years, it's still too often overlooked. I had the good fortune back in 1990 to participate in a series of trainings with the Robin Hood Foundation on impact evaluation, which was more successful in making my agency more fundable than any other step we took. More than that, having the impact data allowed our staff to know whether our approaches were working. We frequently adjusted our approach based on what we learned from the impact evaluations.

Donors and Funders

Closely related to impact evaluation, your donors are very interested in what your nonprofit accomplishes. Donors feel satisfied and fulfilled when they're part of an impactful, substantial, and significant effort, and they want evidence to document it. When you provide this information, you're tending to a key aspect of your multiple bottom lines. You will benefit from a little customization here. Be sure to update your outreach as new stakeholders and supporters emerge.

A transportation museum in Connecticut that I served as fundraising counsel had fifty-plus local and state legislators on their Community Leadership Council. They added those names to their list of constituents and regularly updated them on the museum's performance in attracting visitors and preserving antique vehicles. The legislators responded by issuing occasional million-

---

8 "The Sorry State of Nonprofit Boards," Harvard Business Review, September 2015.

dollar grants to the museum. The State of Connecticut was saying, "We value this museum, and it's better for our region and locality for it to thrive." Paying attention to those legislators and giving them regular updates on the impact of their funds was a bottom line unique to that museum and essential for significant revenue.

Keeping constituencies supplied with impact data will earn you more than just goodwill.

The Bottom Line on Multiple Bottom Lines

High-performing nonprofits understand that engaging, appreciating, and satisfying staff, volunteers, board members, clients, and donors/funders is smart. However, it's crucial to define what bottom-line performance is for each of these areas. Same as with your budget, the performance indicators for each area must be evaluated annually and revised accordingly. You can't just pay attention to net profits and losses.

Some nonprofits have even more bottom lines. It all depends on your circumstances. Ask yourself if you have any other performance areas unique to your nonprofit and include that area as one of your bottom lines.

I acknowledge the complexity of these assessments. *Measuring each bottom-line area, particularly finding common units of measurement, requires the forethought to set performance benchmarks and collect data along the way to show your impact.* This challenge aside, when your organization evaluates its various bottom lines, you will be embracing long-run quality improvement, which will ultimately leave you stronger and more apt to raise significant revenue.

Most importantly, don't grimace like Dominic. Smile instead.

Always remember that a nonprofit has multiple bottoms lines.

13 Cut Costs, but beware of **Underfunding**

The development program is often the first area to be cut or not funded at all. And that's a huge missed opportunity. Statistics bear this out. Beyond the lack of cash, this is largely attributable to leaders not taking enough time to study and think about the fundraising process and the art and science of fundraising.

Knowing how to think about fundraising is the foundation of advanced fundraising and building a robust nonprofit. That's why I wrote this book! And now that you have the heads-up, I urgently ask you to pass on the wisdom!

Quick Test

If you answer "yes" to one or more of these questions, you're underfunding development.

◆ Are you continuously juggling cash flow?

◆ Is your agency's credit line at its limit?

◆ Is your client base growing faster than your donor support?

◆ Have funders asked you for stronger program outcomes, but your quality assurance (Q/A) department is nonexistent or understaffed?

◆ Does your organization need a new program, but you lack planning funds to test it?

◆ Are your investments in techology overlooked?

If you answered "yes" to any of the above, it's not too late to remedy the problem.

The main ideas at play are these:

◆ Nonprofits tend to underfund development to their detriment.

◆ Guidelines about funding development offer numerous measures of how efficient your development efforts are. A workable standard is spending up to 35 percent of each dollar you hope to raise.

◆ There are thought leaders who challenge those guidelines, notable exceptions that we must heed.

◆ If you're trying to reach a new level of fundraising—which you should be—you have to be prepared to spend more and invest meaningfully in your development program.

◆ Be aware of the constraints of your organizational culture, but don't let them impede you.

Missed Opportunities

The many stories I hear about nonprofits underfunding development make me weary. Here are three real cases:

Sarah is the chair of the board's development committee. She considers the youth orchestra to be first-rate, and yet it works very hard to raise its $2.2 million annual budget, while two similar area nonprofits are five times larger. It lacks a fundraising plan because

Sarah doesn't think they can afford the $25,000 it would cost to have a professional come in and work with them to craft one. Its annual budget has flatlined for years, and two of its competitors have transformed their organizations by doing planning.

Similarly, I've spoken with a supposedly cutting-edge nonprofit that provides afterschool programs but has an under-performing website. Its leaders told me they weren't able to afford a redesign. It would cost $25,000 for the format they really need, but they say they just don't have the money. Yet their website is the point of entry for first impressions of the high school kids they're trying to serve.

Then there are the many calls I've taken from nonprofits saying they need more donors and asking how to find new ones. I explain the latest donor research methods available, generally ranging in cost from $18,000 to $55,000, deliver thousands of value-aligned donor prospects (people who already give to missions like theirs and have the financial capacity to give)—a transformational improvement contrasted with the archaic method of purchasing mailing lists and hoping people respond to an appeal. Yet only one in ten nonprofits I have spoken to actually implement this breakthrough, even though the ones that do raise 15 to 20 percent more revenue each year!

How Much Should We Invest?

I empathize with your dilemma, believe me. I'm a frugal guy, and I don't wantonly throw money around. But we can't expect fundraising results without investing in the process and the people required to implement it.

Fundraising is not merely a necessary evil. Dollars spent on fundraising are NOT being diverted from the organization's mission. Spending as little as possible on fundraising is, in fact, unwise and dangerous because you will miss opportunities to fulfill your mission.

Calling for a holistic view of fundraising, a 2017 seminal report, "Measuring Fundraising Effectiveness: Why Cost of Fundraising Isn't Enough,"[9] says this:

> *Investments in effective fundraising strategies should be made not despite our need to fund our missions and work, but because of it. But it is possible to spend too much money on fundraising, and we risk eroding the trust between non-profit organizations and the donors who support us if we ignore that reality.*

The report goes on to describe three primary measures of fundraising effectiveness for both internal and external use, which, taken together, provide a more complete picture of an organization's fundraising health.

Three Primary Measures of Fundraising Effectiveness

Chances are, you'll have a pretty good gut feel for how well your organization's fundraising is doing, just as, when driving a car, you pretty much know how fast you're going.

It's important, though, to make some objective measurements. Doing so not only gives you a snapshot of the current health of your fundraising effectiveness but looking at numbers from prior years gives you a way to spot trends and make sure things are moving in the right direction. And besides your own interest, such measurements will be of strong interest to others, such as staff, board members, and even funders.

Three useful measurements are total fundraising net, dependency quotient, and fundraising efficiency.

---

9 BoardSource, along with its partners at GuideStar, BBB Wise Giving Alliance, and the Association of Fundraising Professionals, released a new framework and calculation for measuring fundraising effectiveness. Jan. 17, 2017: https://trust.guidestar.org/measuring-fundraising-effectiveness-its-time-to-get-it-right

Net Funds Raised

Let's start with the organization's fundraising net, which measures how much money is left to spend on mission after subtracting the cost of fundraising for the measured period. It can be reduced to a simple formula:

Amount Raised – Fundraising Expenses = Net Funds Raised

For example, if your organization raises $2 million in the current year and spends $750,000, its net funds raised is $1,250,000.

Since this formula measures the amount the fundraising program generates for mission, a poor fundraising net that persists for any length of time can not only jeopardize the ability of the organization to pursue its mission, it can jeopardize the organization itself.

This is a good one to track over time. If the fundraising net is trending up, you know your fundraising program is moving in the right direction. If down, well, you need to make changes.

While this sounds simple, making this calculation can be challenging when trying to measure structured gifts such as charitable remainder trusts where, say, the donor retains an income interest for life but commits the trust principal, payable at the donor's death in the form of a remainder interest, to the organization. Measuring these kinds of "planned gifts" often depends on who is doing the measuring, and why. If the organization's accountant is measuring the gift, the gift will typically be booked at the present value of the remainder interest, even though the organization doesn't receive the money until the donor's death. But if it's you as the fundraising professional doing the measuring, you have a decision to make: including this kind of split-interest gift in your calculation before the donor dies (when the remainder interest is transferred to your organization) could be misleading because the money is simply not *yet* available for mission. But not including it underreports the true effectiveness of your fundraising program. In this scenario, I recommend including it but adding a clear notation about the nature of the gift. And be sure to calculate two numbers, one of which includes the value of all gifts including planned gifts where the funds won't be received until a future date, and one that excludes such gifts.

Fundraising Efficiency

It costs something to raise a dollar for your organization. The less it costs, the more efficient your fundraising program is, generally speaking.

You can track fundraising efficiency a number of ways, but the most common is to start with the cost to raise funds in the measured period and divide by the net funds raised, or, to put it into a simple formula:

Cost to Raise Funds ÷ **Net Funds Raised** = **Cost to Raise a Dollar**

We already have, from the example above, our values for cost to raise funds ($750,000) and net funds raised ($1,250,000). All we need to do is use division instead of subtraction to calculate our fundraising efficiency (in other words, the cost to raise one dollar): $750,000 ÷ $1,250,000 = .6, or $0.60 to net $1.00. Stated a different way, the fundraising efficiency is 60 percent.

While it can be useful to compare your organization's fundraising efficiency with that of other organizations, be careful. No two organizations are alike and, depending on their stage of development and a host of other factors, they may well face differing headwinds.

I think it's more valuable, instead, to use this metric in tracking your organization's fundraising efficiency over time. You want to have a trend toward increasing efficiency because you should always be striving to improve the effectiveness of your program.

That said, there will be times when your efficiency decreases for perfectly good reasons, such as when you're experimenting with new approaches or launching a new program. As long as you're aware of this, you will be able to put the calculated number in its proper context.

Dependency Quotient

Does your organization have a broad base of support? If so, congratulations. You could lose some of that support in a given year and the organization would have time to replace the lost funding sources without impacting operations very much, or at all.

Or is it dependent on just a few funding sources and, thereby, vulnerable to losing even one?

Interestingly, if your organization is a 501(c)(3) organization with public charity recognition from the IRS, it's done this kind of analysis at least once—when it asked the IRS to grant it public charity status rather than being designated as a private foundation. The IRS, in making its determination, would have been convinced that your organization is receiving broad enough public support rather than the support of just a few sources; otherwise, your organization would not have been recognized as a public charity in the first place.

Tax law considerations aside, it's important to do this test at least once per year, since the goal should be to move as far as possible away from dependency on just a few funding sources.

One way to measure dependency is to look at your organization's top handful of consistent funding sources. These are the ones who give the largest contributions. If you identify, say, three such funding sources, you can calculate dependency like this: *Total Donated by Top 3 Funding Sources ÷ Organization Expenditures = Dependency Quotient.*

For example, if the top three funding sources gave $250,000 and the organization expends $3 million annually on overall operations, the dependency quotient would be a relatively low 8 percent ($250,000 ÷ $3,000,000). On the other hand, if they gave $2 million, it would be a high 66 percent, indicating a dependency on just a few funding sources.

At this point, it bears repeating that, as I discuss in Chapter 11, while conventional wisdom suggests that a broad array of funding sources is healthier, diversification is often highly over-rated. Even so, it's important, even for those organizations who develop most of their funding from one or just a few concen-trated sources, to measure and assess their dependency quo-tient as a key means of assessing risk and planning for the day when a key funding source stops supporting your organization and must be quickly replaced.

Fundraising Costs Are a Profit Center

Investing in fundraising generates a return. It's a profit center, not a cost center. Yet fundraising costs are not a black hole into which you pour money. Instead, every dollar you spend in fundraising should eventually pay for itself—and bring in multiple dollar returns on your investment.

This means that, according to the Better Business Bureau's Wise Giving Alliance, investing one dollar in fundraising should yield a return of three to four dollars.

Many CEOs starve their development budget and then are unhappy when contributions drop off. Don't be that CEO! Worse, they ignore cause and effect. They fail to understand that if you don't staff the development office adequately, donor cultivation suffers and giving declines.

You may be oversimplifying the question often posed by private foundations: "What percentage of expenses does your organi-zation allocate for fundraising?" The question has trained us to think that spending on development is something to be ashamed of. Clearly, the "right" answer is a low number; but making that assumption all the time would be a grave mistake.

Turn instead to your nonprofit and ask yourself, "How much rev-enue should be devoted to development so that you can accom-plish your sustained mission?" That question is key to avoiding underfunding your revenue program.

The Full Picture

Once you settle on the right approach for funding your development program, the next step is to build your unrestricted operating reserves, which must be part of your organization's unrestricted cash or working capital. Every nonprofit needs to have enough cash flow coming in from various income sources to pay expenses and other obligations when they're due. Some organizations create reserves by setting aside cash in addition to the regular bank fund balances for times when regular cash flow is disrupted.

Reserves are different from restricted funds. Restricted funds are grants and contributions that have been received for specific programs or projects. These funds are restricted according to the grant agreement or the donor's instructions. Sometimes this means that restricted funds sit idle in the bank for a while, and the nonprofit cannot use them for another purpose. Reserves, on the other hand, are unrestricted funds that can be used as the nonprofit's management and board agree. You should have written policies addressing their use and replenishment.

Even Larger Missed Opportunities

You've probably funded capacity and infrastructure costs from your general fund, right? If so, your infrastructure support has usually been underfunded, resulting in missed opportunities to serve your clients and properly support, train, and compensate your staff. You need not have that problem.

Reserves Equal to Three Years

Did you know that a nonprofit can have operating reserves equal to three years of current annual operating expenses? I didn't make that up. The guidance comes from the US Better Business Bureau's Wise Giving Alliance, which assesses whether national organizations follow its "Standards for Charity Accountability." So, if your organization's annual budget is $8 million, you can have unrestricted reserves of up to $24 million. I urge you to aim for the largest reserve possible. Those standards also declare that charities should "avoid accumulating funds that could be used for current program activities."

To raise unrestricted support, as well as to provide additional funding to build infrastructure capacity, you should explore a cash reserve and capacity campaign, in the tradition of capital campaigns. This type of campaign is time-limited, lasting upwards of thirty-six months on average, and seeks special gifts, challenge gifts, and major gifts from your most loyal funders and individual donors, as well as from new value-aligned donors identified through prospect research. These gifts are secured through personal meetings, presentations, and special appeals to funders.

Spending Benchmarks

The Better Business Bureau's standards also recommend that at least 65 percent of the nonprofit's total expenses should be for program expenses and not more than 35 percent for fundraising. That's the broad standard. A nonprofit whose activities are not consistent with its charitable purpose, such as having an exorbitant overhead rate because of executive compensation and expenses unrelated to its mission, might be subjected to an IRS audit, intermediate sanctions, and even the loss of its tax-exempt status.

Charity Navigator, one of the major nonprofit rating services, sets a goal of less than 10 percent of the nonprofit's budget for fundraising spending and considers an organization that spends less than one-third of its budget on program expenses to be failing in its mission.

The standard that fundraisers use when identifying an appropriate cost per dollar raised for annual fundraising is often 25 percent, or $0.25 for every dollar raised. This number has its origins in James Greenfield's *Fund Raising: Evaluating and Managing the Fund Development Process* (1999), which, at that time, noted a 20 percent cost basis. Here is a chart adapted from the book. You might find useful for thinking about the costs of raising a dollar:

Staff Time and Dollars Allocation

Type	Cost to Raise $1	Staff Effort	Dollars Raised
Capital Campaign	$0.05 to $0.10	High	High
Major Gifts	$0.05 to $0.10	Medium	High
Planned Giving	$0.30	High	High
Direct Mail Renewal	$0.25	Medium	Medium
Direct Mail Acquisition	$1.00 to $2.00	Medium	Low
Benefits/ Special Events	$0.50	High	Medium
Grant Writing	$0.25	Medium	Low-Medium
Email/Social Media	$0.01	Low	Low

Please note that even though these statistics are from 1999, I stand by their relevance. For example, the most current data on digital fundraising still has a relatively low return on investment, even though it is going up. There's no doubt that nonprofits should be steadily building the infrastructure for their digital presence. However, the company Growth for Good reported just recently that online display ads had a low return on investment of $0.67 for each dollar spent, and overall social media was $0.97. In short, most nonprofits investing in digital fundraising are not breaking even. In contrast to the other fundraising methods noted above, it still ranks at the bottom. I would recommend nonprofits plan for their development office to keep pace with the proportion of online giving to total private giving. In 2018, $30 billion of the $410 billion raised from private fundraising was through online giving. This is a little over 7 percent and will continue to go up. General guidance can then be that 7 percent of a development staff's time, energy, and resources should go toward building their digital infrastructure for online giving.

Also, these are averages, and there are many variables involved. The most significant variable is your organization's experience with fundraising. Your organizational size matters as well. Larger operations may be able to achieve an economy of scale.

In every instance, these costs should include all direct staff support to conduct the activity.

Contrarian Transformational Views

Consultant and author Dan Pallotta, the fundraiser who invented AIDS and Breast Cancer marathon events, thereby raising millions for these causes, has also done extraordinary work in surfacing the cultural restraints on nonprofit organizations. It's crucial to heed his advice to understand how organizational cultural assumptions and expectations reinforce the tendency to underfund development.

Pallotta argues that charities are discouraged from paying salaries equivalent to those in the for-profit sector and attracting top executive talent. Similarly, nonprofits are not given the same leeway as commercial enterprises to advertise, innovate, experiment, pursue investment capital, and gradually become profitable. There is an ingrained belief, as Pallotta observes, "that overhead is a negative, that it's somehow not a part of 'the cause.'" He adds, "This forces organizations to forego what they need for growth."

Long before Pallotta, the legendary fundraiser Mal Warwick said, "The 'overall fundraising Cost to Raise a Dollar' is a myth. There is NO such standard, and anyone who tells you there is one should survey the real world of fundraising in all its diversity. One organization might be embarrassed to spend more than a dime to raise a dollar, while another might be fortunate to squeak by with forty or fifty cents on a dollar—and both might be ethically run, well-managed organizations." The divergence is caused by different marketplaces, diverse organizational cultures, and varied fundraising approaches.

You Must Decide

My career has shown me that the 35 percent limit for fundraising expenses is a good overall standard; however, there are times when you have to spend more on development, especially if you're trying to break through to a new fundraising level or grow your cash reserves. Don't let existing standards impede you. Instead, I encourage you to think through what investment your organization really needs to prevent underfunding, evaluate constantly to see if it's working, and decide for yourself. Spending just 10 percent of your budget for fundraising/advancement/development costs is absurdly low. Put the plans in place that will help you avoid underfunding and have sufficient revenues to succeed in accomplishing your mission.

Always remember that an easy way to raise money is to cut costs but be aware of underfunding.

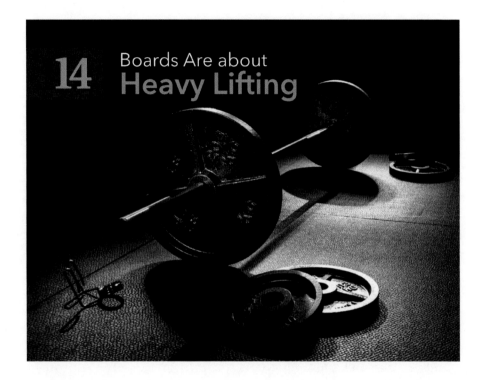

14 Boards Are about Heavy Lifting

A Harvard attorney, Steve was the founding CEO of a thirty-year-old national nonprofit, and he was used to getting his way. His tall stature also helped convey his gravitas. I was mid-sentence when he begged my pardon and said, "That is not my board of directors, Laurence. My board is made up of light-lifters, not heavy-lifters." I went quiet. Everything in me was saying, "No! You need heavy-lifters on your board." Instead, my fundraising training, as well as my contemplative experience, taught me to listen. "Tell me more, please, Steve."

The most frequent question I'm asked is what to do about stagnant boards. "Laurence, they raise no money!" I always turn it around and ask, "How large is your board of directors?" I ask because boards can play a significant role in raising funds. Many states merely require a board of directors to consist of just a chairperson, a secretary, and a treasurer. Yet many, perhaps most, nonprofits have larger boards. A large board can be an effective governance option, and a robust fundraising engine, but not when it's cluttered with board members that are light-lifters. And most nonprofits have boards that are not engaged. How do you address *that* dilemma?

It's better to have just a few people on your board who are willing to put in the time required to get things done and understand the "big picture" of what your organization is really trying to do. I've seen whole organizations transformed by just three or four such people, and it's much more advantageous to recruit this type of board member than a group cluttered with light-lifters.

The Anatomy of Light-lifters

What's a light-lifter? This is the person who comes to one meeting a year and doesn't return the phone calls of the executive director or chief development officer. Light-lifters promise to do something, but you never hear from them. Talking to many such individuals over the years, I've learned that they think along similar lines. They believe their chief contribution to your nonprofit is enabling you to associate their name with your organization. "I'm vice president of XYZ Bank. I'm on your board. Isn't that enough?" They don't solicit their personal contacts. They don't roll up their sleeves. Many don't even include your agency in their own giving. In their DNA, they don't see a problem.

Ironically, light-lifting board members tend to stick around for a long time. This creates a tremendous disadvantage for your organization. Boards full of light-lifters usually remain stuck at the founding stage of organization development.

Three Stages

Overall there are three stages of board/organizational growth: the organizing stage driven by the founder(s), the governing stage driven by the trustees, and the institutional stage where integration between the staff and the board is achieved.

The Organizing Board—Generally informal and relatively passive, this type of board is usually not task-oriented, preferring to rely on a visionary leader (paid or unpaid) to get things done. Alternatively, it may be overly task-oriented to the point of being reluctant to hire paid staff.

The Governing Board—At this level, boards accept responsibility for helping to plan and execute the organization's work. New members are recruited from a variety of professions and, often, higher socio-economic levels. Trustees trust the staff and hold them accountable. Committees are formed for planning, fiscal management, development, and recruiting new trustees.

The Institutional Board—The mature board may be quite large (twenty-five to thirty-five members) and include more people with access to wealth. It has shed outmoded functions and added new ones that fit the profile of the group. Fundraising may become its principal focus—or not. But either way, it usually has a distinct chemistry around which members coalesce. Most of its work is done by committees, including an executive committee to conduct financial and management oversight.

It takes heavy-lifters on a board to progress from the first stage to the second and third. What stage is your board in?

The Heavy-Lifting Board

Heavy-lifters are *engaged*. They are fully engaged with the life and growth of the organization regardless of its stage. They readily apply their skills, talents, connections, and wealth to the pursuit of the organization's mission. Ideally, a board of directors should be thinking about what the organization will look like and accomplish in the next five to ten years. The role of the executive staff is to consider how the organization will function over the next three to five years. A heavy-lifting board grapples with visionary questions like: "How do we define success?" "What do we want to be remembered for?" "What will our work accomplish, and how should we prepare for it?" The most compelling studies of board satisfaction suggest that the happiest trustees are engaged with planning for the organization's future growth and success. That's what they truly want!

The recent collapse of FEGS Health and Human Services—one of the largest social service agencies in the United States, with assets of $144 million, a two-thousand-person staff, 120,000 clients, and 350 locations across the New York metropolitan area—shows what happens when a board fails to undertake long-term planning. Had the board really been engaged in thinking and planning about the organization's future, FEGS would never have had to declare bankruptcy.

I want to emphasize, though, that heavy lifting is more than just fulfilling a task and being alert. When I look back at the boards I've been associated with either as a fundraiser or executive director—boards that spurred the organization forward—I can identify one essential characteristic of the individuals who did the heavy lifting. In different ways and for various reasons, they were all *indispensable*.

How Can You Tell?

The indispensable board member usually can see the direction where the organization must go, even if the odds of arriving there appear to be insurmountable. I fondly recall one board member with an accounting background who reviewed our $650,000 annual budget. "You need revenue for general operating expenses," he told me. "You should apply for government grants that have an overhead cost built in and raise unrestricted private support. That way, you can underwrite the real costs of doing business." I did just that and was able to secure funds for space occupancy, equipment, and administrative staff not tied to specific programs. I did it by talking about our work and where we were headed, not by asking for support for a new copier. That board member helped move the agency to a higher fiscal level. Three years later we were at a $4.1 million annual budget, and 18 percent of those funds were unrestricted. *That's* engagement.

Another board member insisted that we understand our competition and proceeded to do so by investigating other nonprofits in our field and reporting back to me what he learned. I asked him to present the analysis to the whole board, an event that turned out to be a pivotal moment in understanding our service niche and revenue approach. A third board member, trained in group development, devoted himself to ensuring that the trustees work together as a team. He and I would meet monthly over a private breakfast to share our observations about the board as a team—as a small group of people working together. He was the one who initiated private conversations with board members who had missed a couple of meetings and either got them back on track or gently invited them to leave.

Each of these trustees profoundly contributed to bringing our organization to a higher level of functioning. They were indispensable for different reasons, but as a result of their actions, our board meetings became interesting. We even became imbued with a sense of doing something indispensable for the homeless people we served.

The indispensable board members can be identified by what they bring to the table: their own natural strengths.

Cleaning Them Out

When you reflect on who's sitting on your board, and why, you are positioning yourself for institutional advancement and raising more revenue.

Here's an example of how one nonprofit executive separated the wheat from the chaff. She was the CEO of a midsize nonprofit considering a $12 million capital campaign. I was offering fundraising counsel and had interviewed twenty-five donors, including her board members. "Would you agree that your board is full of light-lifters?" I asked. The air in the room seemed to leave. *She* knew the inadequacies of her board, but this was the first time she knew that someone else also knew. As we talked, she saw how her present board curtailed her fundraising. I described the board she could have, the one she deeply wished for.

She already knew that I'm one of the few fundraisers who doesn't expect or require that a board necessarily lead in fundraising.

Instead, I urge clients to examine their board's core strength; if not fundraising, it could be in long-term planning, networking, events planning, etc. That's for the members to decide, per their collective skills and aptitude. But the board has to be a leader in *something*. Otherwise, the agency will never grow beyond the founding stage of organizational development. For a fundraising program to evolve and advance, the board needs to know its core strength, the indomitable strength from which they draw their energy. In her case, it was their expertise about the organizational mission.

Recall that I was there to help her raise funds for a proposed campaign. "There's nothing like a campaign for cleaning out your board," I said. During the next hour we discussed each of the twelve board members, and she saw clearly that four of them had run their course. We decided to meet with the board chair privately to share our thinking and ask for her support.

Fast forward eighteen months into the campaign. The CEO also saw who the indispensable board members were. The light-lifters, the four we had identified, were moved off the board and onto a newly formed Honorary Council, where they could serve in accordance with their own proclivities without retarding the growth of the organization.

Steve, though, never did take my counsel. He retired a few years later, and the organization folded.

Who are the heavy-lifters on *your* board, and what are *you* doing to support them? Which trustees have run their course? What are *your* answers?

Always remember that boards are about heavy lifting. Lightweights need not apply.

15 A Short Definition
for a CEO

J eremy just couldn't make decisions, and his staff was frustrated because of it. At age fifty-five, he had been in three subordinate positions within the organization before applying to fill the CEO vacancy of this caregiver support nonprofit.

Frankly, he really did not evidence leadership traits suggesting he could grow into the position. Jeremy had hired my firm to manage the entire fundraising program. And now even my staff was frustrated with him.

So, I started meeting with him privately. Instead of focusing on Jeremy's weakness, I noticed that within himself he knew where he wanted to head but had not yet developed the executive talents to explain the direction. I decided to work with him on one decision at a time—one strand of spaghetti, not the tangle of the whole bowl. Each week we privately practiced, then he would start the staff meeting by sharing one decision and briefly state the reason behind it. Sometimes he would ask for feedback, sometimes not. These weekly announcements with a detailed action plan revitalized a blasé organization over the next two years. Sometimes the announcements were about small issues, sometimes big.

It is tremendously important for a CEO to make wise decisions. Otherwise, the forward motion of organizational growth will be stalled. While making the best decisions possible is always the aspiration, sometimes we make decisions, then learn more, and a better path emerges. Action can be a great teacher. Which is why CEOs must be adaptable and open to continuous learning, to refining and honing our decisions, and to changing course when necessary.

Many nonprofit boards and executives procrastinate on making decisions. In fact, many nonprofits don't decide much of sub-stance at all—circumstances, or the market, decide for them. In talking with CEOs who are stuck over deciding, they often tell me that they are worried about negative "backlash" once a decision is made. Some say they know what needs to be done but fear the expense of solving the problem correctly. Whatever your circum-stances, if you are having trouble deciding I urge you to get sup-port from someone you trust and who has the right skills regarding the dilemma. I personally speak to at least three experts per situ-ation when addressing the dilemmas my company faces. These conversations often prove to be invaluable for making decisions that move my company to a better place.

Don't let procrastination or indecision ruin your legacy or under-mine your fundraising efforts.

As you read this chapter, see if you can identify protracted dilem-mas within your agency or fundraising program that need to be addressed and apply these ideas to them.

Be Clear at The Outset

Your decision-making process should not be shrouded in mystery. There are, in my mind, three basic approaches to the decisions a CEO makes:

1. **Consensus**: After explaining the dilemma, ask your colleagues, "What should we do?" After setting a few ground rules for listening well, facilitate a robust conversation.

2. **Limited Input**: "I'm thinking about doing this or that but want your input first, and then I'll make my decision."

3. **Field Marshal**: "Here's what we must do and why, and I ask you to follow my direction."

One of my staff members says I tend toward (3) and use (1) or (2) occasionally. Be that as it may, these basic approaches and their attendant questions define my style of making decisions. The first question is like peeling back the layers of an onion—allowing deeper dimensions of the dilemma to emerge from the conversations. In the second instance, you turn to your board, staff, or volunteers and listen—just listen. You conclude by saying when you'll get back to the parties affected, and how. In the third instance, you are directive and clear and ask if anyone needs clarification.

Most people react favorably to the first approach because it builds consensus. My mentor Peter F. Drucker was wary of consensus decision-making, however. He believed that easy consensus indicated that nobody had done their homework. He counseled, "If you have consensus on an important matter, don't make the decision. Wait. Let time work its magic. Let everyone have time to think more." Peter was largely influenced by corporate culture and believed that important decisions made well are always controversial because they point you in a new direction and contradict what has been the norm.

I'm not as wary of consensus, because I was influenced by theological studies and the concept of religious discernment, which is most important in spiritual life. When a parish rector in the Lutheran or Episcopal Church resigns, for example, the church hierarchy doesn't immediately appoint a new one. Instead they appoint an interim pastor, and then he or she facilitates the congregation through an evaluation and assessment process, often six to eighteen months, to make sure they're making the best decision for the congregation.

A forestry agent once told me that in nature, things that grow quickly die quickly; things that take their time to grow last longer. Think of the mighty oak, he said. It grows slowly and lasts a very long time, unlike the birch tree, which grows very fast but has a short life span. Decisions made quickly have a short shelf life. Decisions that endure are ones that you've taken the time to think through.

Being on the Same Page

The popular exhortation that we should all "be on the same page" reflects a bias toward a superficial form of consensus. In reality, a given group of people is never on the same page at the same time. As noted in Chapter 12 ("A Nonprofit Has Multiple Bottom Lines"), the CEO must work to balance the interests of multiple constituencies: the board, clients, employees, and other stakeholders. The CEO has to arrive at a productive approach to each constituency. The three times I was at the helm of a nonprofit, I often pondered how to improve my bottom lines while scanning the horizon for opportunities and threats. If a leader waited for everyone to be on the same page, there would not be any innovation.

The Quakers (The Religious Society of Friends) have an expression: "stepping aside." If someone is blocking a consensus decision, they ask that person, "Can you step aside from blocking the decision without consenting to it?" Asking that question is very sensitive and often allows for a decision to be made in the best interests of the larger group.

One of the most effective decisions Franklin Delano Roosevelt ever made was to gather select corporate leaders together to form a War Production Board to provide the munitions needed by our allies in World War II. He didn't wait for the member CEOs to wander onto the same page. He put them there. Those CEOs were the heads of many of the factories that needed to ramp up production for the war effort. Rather than waiting for consensus, FDR called them to action, and they responded by falling in line.

All three approaches have their time and place.

What Are We Really Deciding, Anyway?

Effective decision-making, rather than the superficial variety, often has to clarify what really needs to be decided. Frequently, the decision that everyone is primed to make is not fundamentally the decision that needs to be made. For example, the board of a major Catholic university thought they had a fundraising dilemma. Do we, they wondered, have the capacity to conduct a $20 million campaign or a $50 million campaign? I counseled them through six meetings, and only the advancement director and I understood that the directors were mulling over the wrong question!

The better question had to do with the donors' views—did the donors agree with the board's notion of how the money would be spent? Interviews with donors revealed they were interested in adult education, specifically retraining workers for twenty-first-century jobs. The board was more interested in moderniz-ing undergraduate academics than in retraining adults and was befuddled on what really needed to be decided.

Telling people what they want to hear is neither good leadership nor good consulting; helping people discern the way forward is. As a CEO, you, too, must perform a consulting role to help your team make the best decisions, and you must ensure that the question being discerned is the best one.

The Decision Process

So, what are the steps in the decision-making process?

1. Do your homework and identify the real problem. Research your competitors and understand their approaches. Evaluate what the naysayers are saying. Comb through the hard data to see what trends you can uncover.

2. Define what must be done to balance and get buy-in from the multiple constituencies involved. Get input from end-users—your clients or customers.

3. Pilot the decision to see where the new direction leads before you get overcommitted. A pilot allows you to see if you're headed in the right direction and to make necessary corrections.

4. Proceed in the new direction with full commitment and proper capitalization.

5. Restate the decision. This is the least obvious step and is often overlooked. People forget the nuances of why the decision was made, or worse, don't see the point of the decision. You have to find ways to reiterate the decision and ask your recalcitrant staffer or board member to explain it back to you. Sometimes, decisions may even be refined at this step. You get compliance when people understand the point of the decision. A simple "Oh," as a shelter resident once said when one of my staffers explained a rule about the use of the laundry room, was enough to quell a contrary impulse.

There are a few common mistakes in doing anything new. One is to go from the idea into full-scale operations. Don't omit the pilot stage. If you do, and skip from concept to the full-scale, even tiny and easily correctable flaws will destroy the innovation.

—Peter Drucker

Perhaps a Paradox

How many big decisions is a nonprofit executive called upon to make, really? *Very few.*

Maybe one to three per year. This is fine. I make this comment after observing hundreds of CEOs up-close over many years. Big decisions change the course of the organization.

Your decision-making energy must be reserved for the BIG things, not the minutia. Smaller decisions should be made by subordinate staff. The major decisions that you should make involve:

◆ Starting a new program

◆ Ending an old program

◆ Pursuing a collaboration

◆ Deciding to raise significantly more money than ever before

When you're called upon to make such decisions, two somewhat paradoxical questions should guide your way forward: *Why are you in such a hurry? What's taking you so long?* Both ends of the continuum are relevant. As I noted above, most nonprofits don't make any decisions at all, let alone the important ones. You want to avoid missing an opportunity through indecision, but your decisions must be informed and well thought out. Have you identified protracted dilemmas within your agency or fundraising program that need to be addressed?

My hope you will apply these ideas and take action. Jeremy stayed on for a successful five years and doubled his nonprofit's annual revenues from $1.2 million to $2.4 million. He still works at making decisions and realizes the unintended consequences of indecisiveness.

Always remember the short definition for a CEO: the one who makes decisions.

The CEO as
Chief Fundraiser

16

"**M**ake it so." No truer words have a CEO spoken, even if the character is fictional. You Trekkers know about whom I speak. Captain Jean-Luc Picard, who first appeared in *Star Trek: The Next Generation,* dramatized the CEO as the iconic leader who says, "Make it so."

I hope you don't think me too weird, but I really did internalize those words in my four CEO positions of nonprofits. I can hear Patrick Stewart utter them and see him in my mind's eye tug down his body-fitting uniform whenever he said them. That's the feeling I hope to transmit to you now as I invite you to unleash your CEO's fundraising power.

You either have to get the CEO out of your way, or more in your way. Choose which is preferable. I've soul-searched over this question for years. In practice, CEOs often restrict their fundraising to the parts of the process with which they're most familiar and comfortable. If they know grants, they tend to focus on that. If they know individual donor solicitation, that's what they focus on. What they generally don't do is ask themselves what revenue sources are most pertinent to their mission and programs.

Rachel Carson, Inc. is a fictitious name for a real national organization. Its mission is to help corporations become more environmentally responsible. It's CEO, Nadine (also a fictitious name), is knowledgeable about corporate giving. She's done very well in this revenue area, but for ten years she's overlooked private foundation giving and individual donor support, as well as earnings that could be generated by fees for service aimed at providing executive training in environmental responsibility.

This is a $2 million organization that could *triple* its budget if resources were invested in developing these three additional revenue streams. Instead, it's remained on a plateau for more than eight years.

CEOs and What They Do

A short definition of a CEO is he or she who makes decisions. The kinds of decisions I'm referring to are the big ones: course corrections—decisions such as those made by the captain of a ship. "We're heading north, but the weather ahead suggests we should turn south."

Usually, three decisions of this order of magnitude face the nonprofit CEO each year:

◆ Do I have the right people on my team?

◆ Do we have enough capital to accomplish what we want to accomplish?

◆ Do we have the right idea about who we are and what we're doing?

To make these kinds of decisions, you need data. You need to know your ROI from present revenue streams and your expected return from potential new revenue streams. What amount of capital must be invested to generate a reasonable return? What's the forecasted return from an incipient grants program or a major gifts initiative? Through higher-level analysis, the CEO integrates "fundraiser-in-chief" into the work of the chief executive officer.

For example, during one of my four tours as a CEO, I contemplated a direct mail campaign. I expected that the initial mailing would pay for itself, but to be sure I reached out to three direct marketing experts to corroborate this assumption. I learned that a first mailing usually doesn't recoup the investment; you must be committed to mailings two, three, and four before the effort pays for itself. If I hadn't checked my assumptions, I would have made a grave mistake. My chief development officer helped me with that research, but it was my job as the CEO to ask the right questions and not act until I had the necessary information to make the best decision.

All staff should have the mandate to recommend high-octane decisions, but it's the CEO who makes them, and necessarily, the CEO must test the assumptions behind the decision and guide the staff through the process of checking their own assumptions.

CEOs and Chief Development Officers

But doesn't the foregoing undermine the chief development officer? The possibility is always there, but both parties need to have the emotional IQ to work out the yin and yang of their relationship. The CEO can't disempower the chief development officer (CDO) and must know when to leave the latter alone. On the other hand, the CDO must know when to bring in the CEO to close out a major gift or help obtain major elements of government support. Both should understand that the CEO has the gravitas and prestige often required to seal a deal. Fundraising is a relationship-building process, and the mere idea of an organization seeking to have a social impact may be too abstract for donors and stakeholders to relate to. Instead, major donors and stakeholders have to have a real relationship with a real CEO.

It's in the contrasting roles of the executive director and chief development officer that the former's position as chief fundraiser becomes crystal clear. The CEO is not only the chief executive officer but is the chief strategic thinker, the thought leader of the organization, and the thoughtful advocate for the organizational vision of a better world. The CEO manages the board and inspires and excites board, staff, and donors about the mission and the work. Everyone else, including the CDO, is involved in the making—the implementation of the strategic fundraising plan. The CEO lives and breathes the bigger picture daily and raises the larger questions, such as: How do we position ourselves to secure a $75,000 award instead of the usual $30,000 gift? What no longer works in our annual fundraising appeal, or, at least, let's ask our donors what they think of it before we launch it? Or, how can we allocate our resources better to raise more funds?

The Secret Sauce

The secret to what really works to help CEOs embrace their role as the chief fundraiser is to engage a coach, specifically, fundraising counsel, to work with him or her. No more effective measure can be taken. I've had half a dozen significant coaches in my career, including the famous Peter F. Drucker. Each one of them helped me advance as a fundraising executive.

Drucker taught me that "Leadership is doing. It isn't just thinking great thoughts; it isn't just charisma; it isn't play-acting. It is doing." *Make it so.* And if you roll that proposition over in your mind, I think you'll easily see why the CEO's role as the chief fundraiser should never be delegated.

What's *your* view of the fundraising role of the CEO, and have you talked with him or her about that recently? Or, if you're the CEO, what can you do to clarify your role and work more harmoniously with your development team? Lastly, if you're the CEO but don't have a development team, try exploring the question of fundraising roles with your development committee or with board members interested in revenue advancement.

Always remember that the CEO is the organization's Chief Fundraiser and that role should never be delegated.

A Dozen Approaches— And That's Okay

The dilapidated conference room with the wobbly table was packed, and the conversation was already heated as forty-plus nonprofit executives crammed in.

The year was 1991. The Red Ribbon symbol took off throughout the world as a symbol of compassion for people living and dying from HIV/AIDS. The legendary basketball player Magic Johnson announced that he was living with the HIV virus and planned to educate young people about how to prevent contracting the virus. It was also the year that rock singer Freddie Mercury of the music group Queen died only a day after he had had announced that he had AIDS.

This was the context in which we nonprofit executives gathered every month. We also responded to additional emergency calls to meet. We did not have to search our missions for "urgency." Urgency was banging our door down with daily death counts!

When I attended those half-day roundtables of senior fundraisers hosted by the Gay Men's Health Crisis in Manhattan, I realized the importance of assessing fundraising talent and matching the right fundraiser to the exact fundraising need.

I usually said very little because I was in rapt observation of how different each master craftsman was in their fundraising approach. Yet they were all wildly successful.

To see their differences displayed in one setting was a unique occasion, and it has stayed with me all these years. It was not merely that each person was different, but that their core approaches for raising millions of dollars varied significantly from one another, partly because of the various organizational cultures in which they worked and partly based on their own past training, mentors, exposure to fundraising theory, and direct fundraising experiences.

Match Fundraiser with Your Unique Need

There is no single way to be a successful fundraiser. Each one of us gravitates toward different types of fundraising, depending on our personalities. One colleague who raises millions every year is, in her own words, "a party girl," and if you need a special event fundraiser, she's the one to hire. Another colleague who also raises millions is more cerebral, and if you want to make sure your strategy is the best it can be, he's the one to pick.

I prefer to design strategies that will substantially grow overall net revenue.

Some fundraisers are entrepreneurial, but many are not. What's important to remember is that there are many different ways to be an effective fundraiser.

Making Your Match

Many of my blog readers write to me when they are ready to hire a fundraiser or when they have just lived through a painful experience with one. Generally, readers want to know what they should do to make the right choice or to figure out what went wrong.

I typically respond with my own three questions:

Question 1: *Is your fundraising dilemma highly entre-preneurial, or is it routine, predictable, and safe?* (I have no bias toward one or the other, and both have their merits and strengths; however, being in denial about which approach you need will surely not serve you.) Explain why you think it's one way or the other. Then ask, what is the fundraiser's predisposition regarding these two polar opposites? Is the fundraiser's skill set a match with your needs?

Peter Drucker saw entrepreneurship as a discipline that could be learned. "Most of what you hear about entrepreneurship is all wrong," he wrote in *Innovation and Entrepreneurship* (1986). "It's not magic; it's not mysterious; and it has nothing to do with genes. It's a discipline and, like any discipline, it can be learned." Further, Drucker viewed entrepreneurship as extending to all types of organizations.

Question 2: *Does your fundraising program have a written plan based on the research about your best revenue sources?* (See Chapter 11 to understand how to determine your best revenue sources.)

Question 3: *How many fundraisers have come and gone from your agency?* But don't stop with this question. Ask, *what did you learn about why they left* and *did you commit to doing anything differently going forward?*

I ask these questions because the assumption behind each forms the basis for a solid fundraising foundation. If answered honestly, your answers indicate whether you understand the nature of your revenue dilemma, if you have thought through how to change it to make your fundraising more lucrative, and whether you have the emotional intelligence to learn from your mistakes and make necessary changes.

When these fundamentals are in place, it's highly likely that the fundraiser will succeed. What are *your* answers to these three questions?

Fundraising Entrepreneurs

Ironically, many nonprofits with nascent fundraising programs have dilemmas that require an entrepreneurially oriented fundraiser. If that's the case, then it may be best to engage a fundraising consultant or fundraising counsel who specializes in diagnosing problems and resolving them.

Many fundraisers know what they know based on their past training, their experience, and their mentors. One fundraiser may have had more exposure to institutional funding (grants), while another has focused on major gifts from individuals. If you need an approach to your fundraising that is different from their past training and experience, they will not be the right fit.

Examples of entrepreneurial organizational dilemmas include breaking out of an over-reliance on government funding or fee-for-service revenue or maintaining revenue while undergoing a leadership succession—or worse, a scandal.

One of my clients, a major healthcare provider, had been without an executive director for more than two years, and their chief development officer had to step up to meet those duties. She received neither a title change to "Acting CEO" nor increased compensation for the extra work. Yes, that shows her dedication and flexibility, but she also had "the constant hunger for making things better and the idea that you are never satisfied with how things are," as Debbie Roxarzade, founder and CEO of Rachel's Kitchen defines entrepreneurship, told *Business News Daily*. She was the right person at the right time.

A fundraiser who has a track record of solving structural dilemmas is likely to be entrepreneurial. Even so, the "entrepreneurial" characterization is overused, especially during interviews, so to truly understand if they are entrepreneurial, you will be better served by asking the candidate to demonstrate the specific ways they've previously made things better.

What Does It Really Take?

My colleague Michael Rosen, author of the bestselling book *Donor-Centered Planned Gift Marketing*, says:

> *If you want to be a successful fundraising professional, you need to constantly expand your knowledge and develop your skills. Great fundraisers are not born. They are created through hard work and dedication. However, if you want to be a truly successful fundraising professional, you'll need more than knowledge and skills. You need passion. You need passion for the profession, your organization's mission, and for improving society.*[10]

Passion, indeed. The word comes from the Latin root *pati* meaning suffering or enduring. Compassion means "to suffer with." The greatest fundraisers I've known empathize with another's pain. That's why they are raising funds, in fact, because they want to reduce the suffering of others. Passionate nonprofit fundraisers seek to ease and eliminate that pain, whether it is from food insecurity and hunger, unemployment and poverty, or any other type of suffering.

I am a fundraiser because I want to do all I can do reduce poverty, the greatest violence. Poverty is defined as a lack of income, but it is also a lack of being nurtured, the key to aspiring to greatness. Knowing what motivates your fundraiser is essential before you hire one.

In addition to determining whether the fundraiser is passionate about your work, you must really document what skills they must have to address your fundraising dilemma, which is critical to helping you hire the right fundraiser. I urge you to make a list of those skills and be specific. Then share that list with a board member and a seasoned fundraiser and get their input.

---

10 Michael Rosen, "Do You Really Have What It Takes to be a Successful Fundraising Professional?" April 8, 2018, https://michaelrosensays.wordpress. com/?s=Do+You+Really+Have.

I once witnessed a national social justice nonprofit hire a major gifts officer who was neither personable nor aware of how to segment donors for a focused fundraising effort. Definitely not the right person for the job! In contrast, I saw another nonprofit, a retreat center, complain that their past development director of six years hadn't raised sufficient annual fund revenues and only brought in planned gifts. In fact, he brought in the most planned gifts the agency ever had, and they were living off of that work from ten years prior! Their ideas of what their fundraiser should do and what he actually needed to focus on to be effective were incongruent. The fundraiser closed so many planned gifts because of the organization's aging donor base. It was the right strategy at the right time. These are two shining examples of why determining the necessary skills you want in a fundraiser must be based on solid data and research.

I also recommend that you have a deep understanding of your prospective fundraiser's individual strengths based on their personality and past training. If you're not sure, have them take a personality indicator test to make an objective determination (Myers-Briggs, DISC, or the Enneagram are all great tools). There must be a strong match between your needs and the fundraiser's talents.

The vetting and interview process itself can also give you a deeper understanding of what type of fundraiser you really need, as opposed to what you thought at the outset. It's better to know and change your mind and approach than to hire and then realize, after the fact, that you don't have the right person.

Many nonprofits hire generalist, can-do fundraisers whose work priorities are scattered to the wind, and whose goals are ill-defined. There may be a right time and place for such an approach, but as your fundraising program matures, you'll need more skilled talent.

With all the different types of fundraisers out there, are you looking for the one that best fits your needs? How do you assess whether your fundraiser fits with the design of your revenue program? Do you have the right match, and can you document why you think that is the case? If you're seeking new fundraisers, have you done your homework beforehand to know what you need, and not just assume that the fundraiser will straighten all that out? You'll be glad you put in the preventive effort to answer these questions at the outset.

Always remember that a dozen development professionals might have a dozen approaches to fundraising, but all can work, and that's okay.

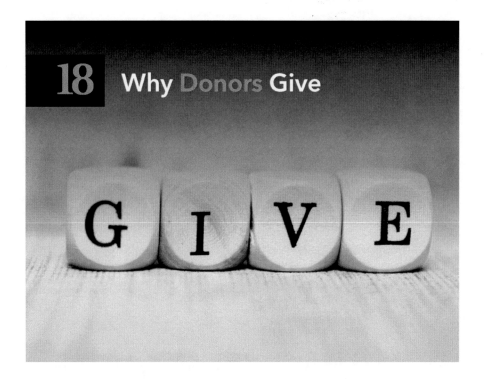

18 Why Donors Give

Maxine, who chaired the gala committee, wanted to invite the famous comedian Whoopi Goldberg to the Lincoln Center benefit concert. Despite advice from our events consultant that doing so would be a waste of time—he knew Whoopi was unlikely to accept—Maxine was insistent. "You never know," she said. I reluctantly mailed the invitation to Whoopi myself.

Later on, our consultant, Robert, privately told me, "This sort of bad thinking is why people foolishly play the lottery." He knew what he was doing. He had filled the house the year before by sticking to inviting those donors who loved us already. In fact, he had given complimentary tickets to some of our highest-end donors who we would meet with in person later on, asking for truly transformational gifts.

To those donors who love your cause, your organization is indispensable. These types of donors are what we call "value-aligned," meaning they share your values, which is critical for a happy partnership. If the donor does not share your organizational values, securing repeat and increased gifts is unlikely.

Donors who are aligned with your organization's values give repeatedly, and as they age, they give away more revenue than ever before. Why? Because older people—even those on fixed incomes—generally have more discretionary revenue because their estates accumulate wealth. Moreover, aging donors want to leave a legacy.

A value-aligned donor needs your organization because they want to be part of making a positive difference. They want to see the homeless housed, the low-income family get a micro-loan to start a business, the struggling farmer get disease-resistant seeds. They want to know that by association with your nonprofit, they've made the world a better place.

Because of their life circumstances, donors aren't able to do what you're doing, but they want to ensure that your work happens.

Peter Drucker said it this way: "People no longer give to charity; they buy into results." In a 1989 interview with Dudley Hafner, then CEO of the American Heart Association, he also famously said, "... fund development is people development."

The Stats

According to Indiana University Lilly Family School of Philanthropy, 55.5 percent of US households gave to charity in 2014, with an average contribution of $2,514 and a median of $900 per household.

But why do they give at all, as opposed to spending the money on themselves?

Reasons for Giving

There are many reasons we in the fundraising industry tell ourselves about why donors give. To name a few: they are moved by the organization's mission, they know a board or staff member, they've given for years. I doubt all of them are true, and I especially doubt they are all true at the same time. Instead, *you must talk to and survey your donors to discover why they specifically give to your agency.*

The number one reason why donors give may sound overly simplistic, but it's true the vast majority of the time—donors give because they are asked! Showing up to ask counts in fundraising.

In a seminal study[11], Rene Bekkers and Pamala Wiepking reported that most people, some 85 percent, give simply because they are asked. They also identified eight mechanisms as the most important forces that drive charitable giving: (a) awareness of need; (b) solicitation; (c) costs and benefits; (d) altruism; (e) reputation; (f) psychological benefits; (g) values; (h) efficacy.

In other studies,[12] donors ranked altruism as their top reason for giving to charity and were more likely to cite it as a factor than reasons that benefit themselves, like getting a tax break. Financial constraint was the only common barrier to giving that donors mentioned.

While these nuances are interesting, the data shows that if you don't ask for support, you're not going to get it. Understanding that will help you win the day.

Frequency Guidelines

Since most nonprofits don't ask often enough—generally just once or twice a year—here are a few guidelines within each communication channel that you should follow to correct that problem.

In general, I recommend at least four appeals per year via direct mail (January, June, November, and December), at least one

---

11 René Bekkers and Pamala Wiepking, "A Literature Review of Empirical Studies of Philanthropy: Eight Mechanisms That Drive Charitable Giving," *Nonprofit and Voluntary Sector Quarterly,* September 10, 2010.
12 Sara Konrath and Femida Handy, "5 Reasons Why People Give Their Money Away—Plus 1 Why They Don't," The Conversation, https://theconversation.com/5-reasons-why-people-give-their-money-away-plus-1-why-they-dont-87801.

email per month, and a weekly social media post of an emotional picture, story, or ninety-second video. For your monthly emails, I recommend a strong story about a single person or cause on which your donors' philanthropy has had an impact, tied to a specific ask.

When someone donates, you must follow up fast to say thank you. While some fundraisers strive for a forty-eight-hour reply, I'm comfortable with sending the note of thanks within five business days. Online donors may be thanked by email immediately following their donation. Mail donors a thank-you letter or a card and use it as an opportunity to start learning more about them. I suggest inserting a five-question donor survey inside the thank-you note with a postage-paid reply envelope. Samples of these surveys are available online.

Most importantly, the next time you appeal to them, you should ask for a donation at an increased giving level! This last point may be the hardest pill to swallow. I know that many of my readers resist asking for increased giving because they do not want to offend their donors. I get that. I don't want to offend them either. Before I get ahead of myself, let me explain a bit more about how it works.

If a donor makes a $15 gift, you would then ask them for a renewal of $25 to $30 the next time you solicit them. You should keep increasing that request generally by 50 percent each time. Both your direct mail house and online platforms can insert algorithms into your correspondence that automatically calculate the increase. This is called "Moves Management," and it's fundamental to securing increased giving. Moves vary in accord with each segment of your donor base.

The originator of Moves Management, fundraiser David Dunlop, wanted to evoke a spirit of generosity in donors to give more.

The goal of Moves Management is that your donors ultimately make a major gift in line with their giving capacity. A "move" is a contact with your donor that builds up his or her loyalty and engagement. Each move is a cultivation step that increases the donor's awareness about your vital work. Consider a "move" a mini strategic plan for each donor.

Fundraisers who use a consistent process to cultivate donors are more likely to achieve their fundraising goals because the more automated those processes are, the better your results. For example, if your agency offers three programs but the donor in question is particularly moved by one of them, it makes more sense to deepen their understanding of how that program works each time you contact them, right? Further, in the context of that deeper messaging, you can ask for increased giving because the more they like the program, the more they will want to support it. Moves Management is not an attempt to manipulate donors; it is trying to influence them to give more in accordance with their interests.

Transformational Donors

As a rule of thumb, the more donors are engaged, the more significant their giving will be. Deeper involvement moves a major donor to become a transformational donor. Larger donors want engagement and partnership within your organization and should, therefore, be invited into your governance and planning.

Think about philanthropist Michael Bloomberg and his recent $1.8 billion gift to Johns Hopkins University, the largest gift to date to a US college or university. An alumnus, his support will fund undergraduate financial aid and allow Johns Hopkins to be a loan-free institution. All undergraduate student loans will be replaced with scholarships, and family contributions to tuition and expenses will be reduced. Also, immediate loan relief is being offered to every enrolled undergraduate student whose financial aid package includes a federal need-based loan.

As a generation of young adults is drowning in student debt, this is truly a transformational gift; but be assured that Mayor Bloomberg needed Johns Hopkins as much as they needed him because he could not have solved the problem of training the best healthcare professionals on his own. He needed to affiliate with a storied nonprofit educational institution to do so. An extraordinary example of shared values, Bloomberg's combined philanthropy to Johns Hopkins exceeds $3.35 billion, and his total philanthropy exceeds $6.4 billion.

Finding Your Donor's Motivation

As I noted above, it's crucial that you talk to and survey your donors to discover why they specifically give to your agency.

Here are some examples of nonprofits I have worked with who took this step, and what they discovered:

A support organization for parents whose child has cancer found that the fact that the organization's board and staff were 100 percent comprised of parents whose child had endured cancer made them trust completely in the organization and donate generously.

A faith-based treatment center for men found that the families trusted the staff more because they knew the priests and brothers of the religious orders and trusted them implicitly. The fact that 72 percent of the graduates stayed sober was interesting but not as much as the personal connection with the clergy.

A soup kitchen where I served on the staff for many years found that their donors were inextricably linked to those who volunteered at the soup kitchen. Treating the volunteers well and giving them the support they needed was directly tied to increased fundraising.

What are *your* donors' motivations for giving? Are you seen as indispensable to at least your largest donors? What can you do to make your motivations and impact clearer to your donors?

Loving an organization's cause and buying into the results of its work are the primary factors that drive my own giving. To find out your donor's motivations, you must ask them thoughtfully and listen well.

Whoopi, by the way, hosts the Comic Relief television specials benefiting charities helping the homeless. She was also named a UNICEF Goodwill Ambassador in 2003 and serves on the board of Garden of Dreams. She did not attend our gala, though, just as Robert had predicted.

Always remember that donors give for many reasons, but especially because they love your cause, and they need you to make the difference they want to see in the world.

19 Giving at All Levels is Major

Twenty-eight years ago, when I was the CEO of a large non-profit, a modest gift arrived from a donor who I had hoped would give more. My chief development officer saw my frown, closed my office door, and sat down. "Laurence," he said, "every gift, no matter the size, is important. He didn't have to give us anything."

I recall the sting of that lesson often. That day, I learned about gratitude—particularly my lack thereof! That experience showed me that giving at all levels is major, even though fundraisers are trained to qualify major donors as the top 20 to 30 percent of those who give the most.

Before we get ahead of ourselves, let's review the basic giving segments.

There are many ways to segment donors. I like these six the best:

Bread & Butter Donors are those who give $1 to $999. Once these donors make a first gift, we should invite them to join a monthly giving program.

Lead Donors are those who give $1,000 to $5,000 annually. They, too, can be part of your monthly giving program, but you have to survey them and ask them if they want to join.

Major Donors are typically those who give $5,000 and up annually. Depending on your donors' capacity, however, $5,000 may be too low of a threshold. To figure out the giving amount that defines your major donors, segment the top 20 to 30 percent of all your donors and then see what that giving range is. That range defines your major donors. It may not be a range that you like or want to maintain, but it is your starting line. Use it as a benchmark.

Capital Donors usually give $10,000 and above and are those who often make multiple-year pledges three to five years in length that are dedicated to reserve funds, endowment funds, and various special projects like building funds.

Transformational Donors are those six-figure donors whose gifts transform the very field of service your nonprofit is dedicated to. Often referred to as "mega-donors," their ultra-high net worth also brings the advantage of their social capital—their reputations and business connections—in addition to their own private funds, to find solutions for causes about which they deeply care. And many times, other donors of that same caliber follow in their footsteps.

Planned Giving/Estate Donors are those who remember you in their Last Will & Testament or establish a financial instrument through life insurance or a charitable remainder trust and designate your nonprofit as the beneficiary. According to Michael Rosen's substantial *Donor-Centered Planned Gift Marketing*, while only 5.3 percent of those over age fifty have made a charitable bequest commitment, 33 percent of Americans are willing to consider a charitable bequest. This means that there is a great deal of untapped potential.

By saying that all giving is major, we're setting a standard that no matter the size of the gift, just the fact that the donor has given to you is significant. This standard insists that the donor's viewpoint wins the day.

I ask donors to give what, for them, is a gift of significance. By significance, I mean that it's among their top three largest gifts that year. If that's not a major gift as the donor defines it, I don't know what is.

80/20

Make no mistake—I realize that 80 percent of your fundraising will likely come from 20 percent of the donors who have the capacity to give. (I spoke of this principle in my last book, *The Nonprofit Fundraising Solution*.) Also known as the Pareto Principle—named after its founder, the Italian economist Vilfredo Pareto, in 1895—this rule proposes that 20 percent of your activities will account for 80 percent of your results. We fundraisers apply Pareto's 80/20 rule to major gift fundraising, and we align our time to work with the 20 percent of those potential donors with the capacity to make major gifts. Understanding this principle is essential to aligning your major gift program with how you can most effectively spend your time.

Oseola McCarty

Keeping Pareto's rule in mind, there is nonetheless significant power in the 80 percent of your donors who may not make large gifts but whose impact can be just as important. Nothing demonstrates why all donors are major donors more than Oseola McCarty who, living in a simple frame house, built a small fortune one and two dollars at a time taking in laundry and ironing. Despite her humble life as a washerwoman, she donated her life savings of $150,000 to a scholarship endowment for poor Mississippi students. When he learned of this amazing example of philanthropy, Ted Turner gave away a billion dollars.

Is the Principle of Proportionality Limiting Your Large Gifts?

With these various types of donors in mind, you must understand another key fundraising principle—proportionality.

Have you ever wondered why you're not getting larger individual donations or funder awards? It is perplexing, isn't it? You did your research, and you know that the donor/funder makes larger gifts, but they haven't made them to your agency, which is frustrating! You wonder, "Was it how I asked? What happened?"

Generally, the answer to this question is rooted in the principle of proportionality. In fundraising, the principle of proportionality is the understanding that a donor/funder's giving is in proportion to the whole, a donation amount made at the "right size," if you will. Proportionality is often at work, and you must be aware of it.

In my experience, most donors or funders give in proportion to your annual budget or campaign goal size, at no more than 10 percent of the goal. So, for example, if your annual organizational budget is $750,000, you can expect that the largest gifts and awards will be around $75,000. Proportionality is the cold, hard reality that's rarely discussed, yet it's the elephant in the room! Of course, there are plenty of welcome exceptions, but they're not the norm.

Just recently, a major foundation funder told me privately that it would only make a $20,000 grant to one of my clients, even though we had asked for $45,000 and really needed the full amount to hire a new staff person. When I politely inquired as to why it would not consider the full grant, he said it was because the small number of clients served (forty at a time in an overnight shelter) and the overall program budget of $220,000 did not warrant a gift of that size. Proportionality was at work. Further, the fact that the request was for expanded services over and above the $220,000 budget did not matter!

Donor Expectations

Another aspect of proportionality is to consider whether the donor's expectations of what your nonprofit will deliver are in sync with the size of the gift. As you get to know a donor, you develop an understanding of his or her motivations and expectations for giving. According to the Council of Advancement and Support of Education, a good fundraiser will gently manage the expectations of a donor prospect during the cultivation and solicitation process, both to ensure that they are compatible with the institution's capacity to deliver and are proportionate to the size of the proposed gift.

For example, a modest donor giving $1,000 to support scholarships cannot expect a private dinner with the vice-chancellor and monthly meetings with the scholarship program director. However, the donor might expect an invitation to an annual scholarship awards ceremony, a written note of thanks from one of the recipients, and a yearly report on the progress of the funded scholars.

It's vital that at the point of solicitation both the fundraiser and the prospect have the same understanding of the level of stewardship that is appropriate for the gift. For more substantial donations, written gift acceptance and recognition agreements are warranted. For annual fund appeals to your bread-and-butter donors, the appeal material should state upfront the level of stewardship a donor can expect. For example, donors below $1,000 might expect a certificate, a bumper sticker related to the organization's mission, or a thank-you phone call or text at Thanksgiving.

You might also find it useful to set some internal stewardship guidelines. Start with the basic level of stewardship that entry-level donors should expect (e.g., the gift processed, and the receipt issued, within five working days, a written "thank you" within seven working days, an annual report via email, etc.). Your agency should develop ranges of stewardship relating to different levels of giving. That's where a stewardship matrix will serve you well.

Consider a Stewardship Matrix

A stewardship matrix is a grid used to determine what type of acknowledgment and reporting each donor receives about a gift. This matrix is typically segmented based on your target donor groups, and you can make it as general or detailed as you like. On the opposite page is a sample stewardship matrix that I've found useful.[13]

I encourage you to use this model and make your own matrix that fits your development program.

Your stewardship guidelines must be flexible, as some funders will have their own reporting requirements, and major donors may have their own ideas of how they want their relationship with your institution to develop. Having a set of guidelines will help you design appropriate stewardship strategies that you can fulfill, even with limited resources, and treat all of your donors with the importance and recognition they deserve.

Treating All Donors as Major

Osceola McCarty once said, "There's a lot of talk about self-esteem these days. It seems pretty basic to me. If you want to feel proud of yourself, you've got to do things you can be proud of. Feelings follow actions." She deserves our esteem both for her own philanthropy and as illustrative of the 55.5 percent of Americans who donate to charity annually, averaging $2,514 per household.[14]

There is likely to be an Osceola among your donors. How are you taking action to treat him or her as significant? He or she did not have to give you anything.

Always remember that a major gift can be $10 or $100,000. Giving at all levels is major.

---

13 Training Resources for the Environmental Community stewardship matrix, which shows a way to provide increasing levels of stewardship and personal connection as donors give more. See https://www.trec.org/wp-content/uploads/2015/02/Stewardship-Matrix_v818.pdf.
14 Lilly Family School of Philanthropy: Philanthropy Panel Study https://philanthropy.iupui.edu/research/current-research/philanthropy-panel-study.html

Sample Stewardship Matrix

Stewardship Activity	Up to 9 (Monthly)	up to 99 (One-time)	10-29 (Monthly)	100-299 (One-time)	30-49 (Monthly)	300-499 (One-time)	50-99 (Monthly)	500-999 (One-time)	100-199 (Monthly)	1,000-2,499 (One-time)	200-399 (Monthly)	2,500-4,999 (One-time)	400 & up (Monthly)	5,000 & up (One-time)	Bequest
Special Invite													×		
Stewardship Trip												×	×		×
Card or Call											×	×	×		×
E.D. Handwritten										×	×	×	×		×
Special Newsletter										×	×	×	×		×
Quarterly Major Donor											×	×	×		×
Phone Call from BOD								×	×	×	×	×	×		×
Major Donor Event								×	×	×	×	×	×		×
Small Gift (Calendar, Magnet, etc.)							×	×	×	×	×	×	×		×
Personal Email							×	×	×	×	×	×	×		
Print Newsletter		×	×	×	×	×	×	×	×	×	×	×	×		
New Donor Welcome Packet	×	×	×	×	×	×	×	×	×	×	×	×	×		×
Acknowledgement Letter	×	×	×	×	×	×	×	×	×	×	×	×	×		×
Gift Amount	×	×	×	×	×	×	×	×					×		

Donor Type row: Monthly, One-time, Monthly, One-time, Monthly, One-time, Monthly, One-time, Monthly, One-time, Monthly, One-time, Monthly, One-time, Bequest

Chart courtesy of Training Resources for the Environmental Community
© TREC https://www.trec.org

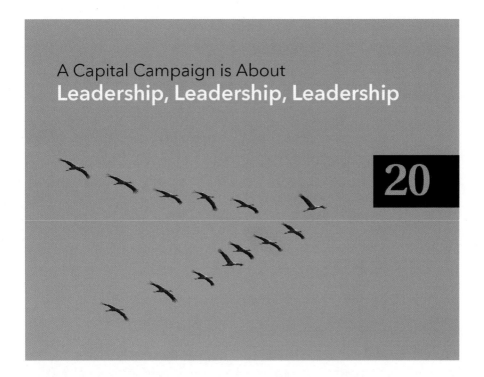

A Capital Campaign is About
Leadership, Leadership, Leadership

20

John had never asked for even as much as lunch money before, let alone $6.5 million. As the board chair of a Quaker-sponsored affordable housing project, he asked me to breakfast to learn about how this thing called fundraising worked. I asked him, "Are you a leader?" Without hesitation, he said, "It depends on the circumstances." I liked John right on the spot.

A fundraising campaign comes alive because of key leadership comprised of carefully selected volunteers, the right fundraising professional (staff or external campaign counsel), and donors who are willing to step up and share their passion for your organization's mission. Those three human resources are the keys to campaign success.

An overwhelming amount has been written about capital fundraising campaigns—how to run one, the role of a feasibility study, the various stages of how a campaign unfolds, and why the case for support is so important—just to name a few common themes. There's even a new genre of "campaign templates" that proposes making campaigns more "boilerplate" and not as customized as we've traditionally thought necessary. You can read that content online and within the usual fundraising industry books; in fact, I have been among those writers.

What has not been addressed in the current literature, however, is the serious dearth of fundraising leaders, especially for major campaigns. In days of old, corporate captains of industry and their wives often filled these roles.[15] Some still do, but in a world where income inequality is ever-increasing, corporate leaders are often seen as part of the problem.

In this chapter, we'll discuss this crisis of fundraising leadership, and I'll suggest ways to respond to that dilemma.

Calling Forth Leaders

Rallying leaders to action has always been necessary, but it is even more imperative in an age as individualistic as ours. Asking volunteers to step up and lead shows that you have confidence in their willingness and ability to support the community. Having a specific plan for engaging potential volunteer leaders is always a good idea, but you should also be prepared to listen and discover how they want to be involved, if at all.

What happens when you don't have the right volunteer campaign leader in place? Too often, nonprofit CEOs suffer in silence, keeping their concerns hidden. Instead, I suggest bringing your need for effective leaders to the forefront of your campaign planning and asking other stakeholders to help you find and engage the real volunteer talent you need for a successful campaign that will move donors to give.

According to nonprofit CEO Susan N. Dreyfus:

> *Social scientists have long noted that volunteerism plays a significantly larger role in American civic life than it does in*

---

15 See Dan Pallotta, *Uncharitable* (Lebanon, NH: University Press of New England, 2010) for an excellent history of how the nonprofit sector developed.

other countries. In fact, Americans are 15 percent more likely to volunteer their time than the Dutch, 21 percent more likely than the Swiss, and 32 percent more likely than Germans. And yet, despite these statistics, they have begun to raise alarm bells about a decline in US volunteerism. According to the Bureau of Labor Statistics, volunteerism peaked between 2003 and 2005, when 28.8 percent of Americans reported having volunteered the previous year. Today, that number is 25.3 percent. This decline is consistent across every single age and education group, representing a loss of millions of volunteers. What's more, as the number of volunteers has decreased, the need for them has grown. The nonprofit sector, which relies heavily on volunteers as a strategic resource, has grown by 25 percent in the past decade, according to researchers.[16]

Clearly, then, fundraisers must do more to recruit talented volunteers to lead our important work. But what should we look for in a leader?

Traits of Top-shelf Campaign Leaders

The qualities that define a leader are numerous and wide-ranging, but when it comes to capital campaigns, here are some specific traits I have seen in the best campaign leaders:

◆ **Priority**: They make the campaign a priority and put in more time and energy than other stakeholders.

◆ **Reform Plan**: They've thought deeply about the institution's need for organizational reform—not just the need for revenue—and have a plan in mind beforehand that describes the changes needed for a successful campaign.

◆ **Financial Giving**: They lead by making their own gift, one that is significant and among the largest of their lifetime charitable gifts.

---

16 Susan N. Dreyfus, "Volunteerism and US Civil Society," *Stanford Social Innovation Review,* Aug. 29, 2018, https://ssir.org/articles/entry/volunteerism_and_us_civil_society.

◆ **Confidence**: They foster confidence that the work can be done and will succeed, even as they acknowledge difficulties.

◆ **Thoughtful Challenges**: They express challenging ideas to other stakeholders and do so in a timely and thoughtful way that allowed their ideas to be well-received.

◆ **Private Time**: They use private conversations to learn more about other stakeholders' views, and to share their own, in a way that a group setting doesn't allow.

◆ **Revenue & Leadership**: They realize they have the mandate to bring in more revenue, but also know that leadership is even more essential than ever.

◆ **Gratitude**: They express gratitude constantly as part of their way of managing the campaign.

◆ **Listeners:** They learn to listen well to the donor, especially after asking for a gift.

Did each leader exhibit these traits all of the time? No. Was coaching required to help them actualize these traits? Yes. The point, however, is that we fundraisers have to set the bar for what campaign leadership requires. We have to understand and be able to describe the traits we're looking for with our development committee and trustees and use a list like this to vet our possible campaign leaders.

I realize that many fundraisers are not, unfortunately, necessarily empowered as change agents within their organizations. Being able to influence the culture of an organization is essential to calling forth leaders and empowering existing ones to fundraise at higher levels. In fact, I have encouraged top-notch fundraisers to leave their positions because the obstructions they faced were insurmountable.

I realize that few of us ever start capital campaigns with a clean slate. Instead, we often have to work with the leaders we have. Sometimes the existing team can be enhanced by recruiting new leaders, and if that's the case, here's how to identify and recruit them.

How to Identify and Recruit Leaders

Overall, I have found the adage "Look for the people who get things done" to be true. Those doers are usually very busy people, too, which means fundraisers may overlook them, thinking they will say "no" to your request because of how busy they are. This may seem counter-intuitive, but busy people generally have lots of organizing systems in place and enjoy using their networks to help your cause. In other words, they're busy because they thrive in that environment, so I encourage you to put that hesitation aside and explore working with them.

Outside of that broad rule, here are a few unique ways I have found new leadership talent.

Wealth Screens

Did you know that you can find new high-level volunteers by wealth screening your donor database? Donors who are already affiliated with nonprofits are tagged in any wealth screen you purchase, and that affiliation has usually been in a leadership role. In one recent case, a faith-based treatment center, we found sixty-seven new prospective leaders who had served on other nonprofit boards, reached out to them, and were able to recruit two new volunteers as development committee members.

Simultaneously screening a prospective donor list is an adjunct strategy to wealth screening your current donors. Such a list is created by your data vendor based on value-aligned affiliations that match your nonprofit—things like giving to similar charities, living near your service area, and giving capacity. The new list will also show you who is already affiliated with nonprofits, which typically indicates experience in a leadership role.

Major Gift Meetings

When you're in a major gift meeting, ask the donor if they would like to serve on a board or organizational committee, assuming you think they have the skills you want. Starting a new volunteer off with a specific committee assignment, instead of bringing them onto the board or campaign cabinet right away, allows you to get to know them and assess whether they're a good fit for campaign leadership. That's an essential precautionary step that should last at least a year; then you can evaluate the best next step.

Join a Local Professional Association

I once recruited three new members for one nonprofit's corporate council by joining the local Chamber of Commerce. The fee was $250, and the agency I was representing paid it as part of its development office direct expenses. It sure got its money's worth—those three members chaired its next gala committee and raised the net income of that event from $250,000 to $610,000!

In addition to Chambers of Commerce, I've found Junior Leagues to be a terrific resource, as well as Rotary Clubs and Kiwanis Clubs. Catholic fundraisers have had success among the Knights of Columbus and the alumni associations of their colleges, and Jewish colleagues have found talent in the up-and-coming ranks of the Young Jewish Professionals Network. Local professional associations whose values align with your organizational mission are an excellent source for connecting with new potential leaders.

Hire a Search Firm or Consultant

Using a reputable search consultant can help you find highly qualified leaders. The fee for this service is usually reasonable. One such consultant I worked with charged $5,000 per search for a new trustee, and she found excellent leaders. While there are no guarantees that the person who was recruited will last, the cost of doing nothing or going about the search process without expert resources was a far greater risk!

FAQs of Campaign Leadership

What happens if my campaign leadership isn't getting the job done?

I have often been asked at my blog, INFO, if volunteer leaders can be fired. Yes, they can if it's not working out. If you're faced with a leader who isn't meeting your organization's needs, you should try to have a thoughtful conversation, or even an exit interview conducted by a neutral third party, so that an airing of issues can occur and you can avoid replicating the same problems going forward. Ideally, you should strive to reorient the person to a role within your organization that is better suited to the person's interests and talents.

Is a fundraising-oriented leader different from a generally good leader?

Yes. Both share many traits in common, but the fundraising leader you need for your campaign sees philanthropic giving as the *raison d'être*. This doesn't make the fundraising-oriented leader better than anyone else, just different—oriented toward seizing an opportunity rather than being risk-averse. Great fundraising leaders often make other leaders nervous because they focus on action more than process. Of course, we need a healthy mix of both, but action is critical to raising large sums. Fundraising leaders prefer *doing* first, *evaluating* second, and then *doing* even better.

How would you describe the ideal relationship between the lead fundraiser and the executive director?

Finally, the question I'm asked the most concerns the relationship between leaders, particularly that between the primary fundraiser—the campaign chairperson or co-chairs—and the CEO. My answer: a true partnership between the executive and fundraising leaders is necessary to achieve a successful campaign. So many fundraising efforts fail because this partnership is not real. I described in Chapter 16 that an executive director must be an active participant in fundraising. If you believe that a chief development officer or campaign co-chair is solely responsible for raising money, you are in for a rocky and challenging campaign. All leaders involved with major fundraising must be in sync, honor one another's style, and work in a complementary and collaborative fashion. That's what it takes to have an effective capital campaign.

At the start of this chapter, I referred to the dearth of campaign leadership as a crisis. In every crisis lies an opportunity, depending on how you think about it. The choice before you is to choose the right leaders for your campaign and be proactive about how you do that. The tips above come from my own efforts, and I encourage you to add to that list in your fundraising.

My Quaker client, John, helped us raise a lot of funds, and we did finish the $6.5 million campaign. He grew through the process, and so did I. Once, John quoted another famous John: "If your actions inspire others to dream more, learn more, do more, and become more, you are a leader." —John Quincy Adams. I liked that John, too.

Always remember that a campaign is defined by its leadership. A campaign is leadership, leadership, leadership.

ROI Is Not Just a Math Exercise

21

ROI? I usually avoid jargon, but these three letters, well, I just love 'em. And you should too! ROI means the return on investment. This calculation shows the number of dollars raised compared to the amount spent on fundraising services. You should take this important performance measure seriously.

Understanding the results of your nonprofit's ROI analysis allows you to adjust your fundraising to focus on the revenue areas of greatest return. Yet, most of us use the same fundraising methods year after year, neglecting to correlate our precious time with the most lucrative activities.

But please be careful not to fall into the trap of thinking of ROI as just a math exercise. Fundraising is not all mathematics. It's about people and relationships and having the right processes in place. There are a lot of moving parts to it, and they can't all be measured in the same way.

What Can Be Measured?

Let's talk first about what can be measured. To calculate your ROI for, say, private and corporate foundation grants, you simply divide the total amount of awards received by your fundraising expenses for that work. So, for example, if you raised $270,000 in grants at the cost of $40,000 for the grant writer, your ROI was $6.75. Your board report would state that: "We have raised $6.75 for every dollar we spent on grants work in the past year."

According to the Maryland Association of Nonprofits' Standards for Excellence and other credible sources, an established ROI benchmark for high-efficiency nonprofits is three to one, or three dollars raised for each one dollar spent on fundraising. A return of $6.75 would be fantastic.

ROI can be computed for each aspect of your fundraising program so that comparisons can be made. Then you can combine each part and determine the total ROI is for the entire fundraising program.

Note well, however, that you can successfully spend a full year getting ready to raise funds and not secure a dime. The "getting ready" phase, unfortunately, is not generally appreciated, which is terribly frustrating for development professionals. If you anticipate such a trajectory, finding an underwriter for the fundraising expenses in your first year would be worth exploring. Underwriting of development costs usually comes from a trustee or current donor interested in capacity building.

Getting Ready

The truth is, the most lucrative activities a fundraiser can undertake usually require the most preparatory time. Take, for example, planned giving—a process involving your donor's estate plan. Securing a planned gift often requires one or more meetings with donors and, possibly, walking them through a menu of intricate financial instruments. (Please be aware that planned giving is not as unattainable as many fundraisers think, especially since 85 percent of planned gifts derive from a simple sentence you can insert on your website: "Remember us in your will.") I know of a non-profit that was almost forced to close its doors until an enormous planned gift was received. That gift was the result of work done by the previous development consultant—by the way, a person the board had determined wasn't very effective! "How do you feel about him now?" I asked them.

Complex government grant applications also require significant preparatory time, but they sure can be lucrative. While most high-functioning private grant programs return $3 to $4 for every dollar spent on them, a government grant program can return $27 or more for every dollar spent. Government grants are huge applications spanning in length from sixty-five to over two hundred pages, requiring online submissions at wonky government portals. Further, extensive research must be done *before* applying to make sure that your mission is a solid match for what the government agency is offering. On occasion, I've spent a week vetting a government request for proposals to find out if it's a good fit for my client—only to advise my client to walk away from the application!

Forging real partnerships with other nonprofits is another example of work needing preparatory time, yet such partnerships are vital to the mission and effectiveness of nonprofits. They can also substantially help raise revenue. The Bridgespan Group defines nonprofit partnerships as "strategic alliances between nonprofits that are intended to achieve greater impact than any organization could generate on its own."

My teacher, Peter F. Drucker, used to say that "Partnerships are difficult, period; but essential in the modern world." Your non-profit needs to know and coordinate with other nonprofits with similar missions so that your work can be synchronized and avoid duplication.

When I worked in Richmond, Virginia creating housing for home-less people, we formed a city-wide coalition of more than a dozen providers and wrote a master plan for addressing and preventing homelessness that was ratified by the Richmond City Council. Our partnerships vastly moved the needle on improving the conditions of the homeless and brought us a lot more revenue, buildings, and even new state-wide legislation to fund our work than we had when we stood in silos. For example, three of the coalition members came together and filed an application to the Department of Housing and Urban Development (HUD). We mailed off a huge crate of forms and attachments following a week's worth of work. The funding request was for a three-year mobile mental health pilot program at the cost of $210,000 per year. To our delight, HUD funded the entire program.

Of note, building significant partnerships with other nonprofit agencies makes your organization *appear* substantially bigger than it actually is. The funder's perception is a major part of fundraising. If you appear bigger, you'll be able to apply for and receive larger private grants or secure more significant corporate sponsors. That's essentially what we did in Richmond with HUD.

Reevaluating Priorities

Yet I find that many nonprofit partnerships are often shallow, and not enough effort is put in to make them real. Why is that? I realize that the demands of modern life tend to leave us scattered, but when you look at how real partnerships benefit the clients we serve, it's worth reevaluating our priorities.

The merger of two youth service organizations in New York City—Groundwork and the Edwin Gould Academy—with Good Shepherd Services (GSS) is a case in point. GSS acquired two smaller nonprofits. The first propelled the agency into the high-need neighborhoods of East New York and Bedford-Stuyvesant. The second brought a supportive housing residence for homeless youth aging out of foster care and juvenile justice programs. Multiple benefits were derived from this merger beyond the obvious benefit of expanding to a new neighborhood. One of those benefits included the chance for the executive staff to really rise to the occasion and live what they had been trained for. They came together as a powerful team.

In her article "5 Tips for Nonprofit Collaborations," published by The National Council of Nonprofits, Jennifer Chandler observes that:

> *grant makers frequently encourage nonprofits to collaborate but don't recognize the costs—and therefore don't provide funding to nonprofits that they are simultaneously urging to collaborate...Grantmakers also should remember that achieving real results from collaborative efforts can take time.*[17]

Exactly.

All-Important Process Outcomes

A final word about measuring your return on fundraising: I consider *process outcomes* just as important as the mathematical measurement of ROI. What are process outcomes? These are the steps you have to take to be ready to fundraise. They can include:

1. Writing a compelling *case for support.* In writing the case statement, you must explain the business assumptions behind your need for revenue and the urgency of acquiring those funds. Writing the case statement could take a few weeks or a few months. One case statement I wrote took a *year* to complete. I would not typically recommend that, but it was worth it; it brought in a lot of revenue, assuring the success of the campaign.

2. Getting your *database in shape* so that you have accurate donor information—this is called "data hygiene" among fundraising wonks.

3. *Surveying your donors* once a year. Surveying donors lets you discover what interests *them* and how they prefer to be communicated with. The information obtained from the survey can then be entered into each donor's record and acted on as necessary.

---

17 https://www.councilofnonprofits.org/thought-leadership/5-tips-nonprofit-collaborations

4. *Training your volunteers* to get them ready to solicit and cultivate donors.

5. Having a *development audit.* If you lack a solid fundraising plan, an audit will identify your strengths and weaknesses, and enable you to create a plan that builds on your strengths and addresses your weaknesses.

6. *Shoring up your board* to get people on it who have substantial personal networks and connections to wealth. One of the main, if subtle, differences between high-powered museums and universities on the one hand, and high-performing but under-resourced community nonprofits on the other, is the nature of the people sitting on the board. The board of the Metropolitan Museum of Art consists of the city's movers and shakers; the board of Youth on the Move, Inc., is made up mostly of social workers. Yes, it's nice if the composition of the board reflects the community, but it's better if one or two of the trustees can pick up the phone and get a prominent banker or financier to attend your gala. Of course, it takes time and effort to recruit such trustees.

Spreading the News

Once you have calculated your ROI, don't hide your light under a bushel. Cast it for all to see! Prepare a report—a one-page version is just fine—to share the details of your return with your board and select donors, preferably the major donors. Having such a report is an excellent way to engage leadership in a deeper dialog, plus it could present an opportunity to ask donors for increased support if the timing is right.

The most important question that needs to be answered is: "What are we doing to have a better ROI next year?" Tomorrow will be here in the blink of an eye. The things you need to do to get ready for an increased return on your fundraising investment have to be attended to *now*.

Both Sides of the ROI Coin

"Laurence, I agree completely with what you say about ROI and the process elements. But nobody at our agency thinks about it, and, when they do, all they think about is the math."

I've heard this dozens of times, and I fully understand why people look at the math first. That's human nature. But I urge you to consider the concept of ROI in all its dimensions.

My associates and I once spent a year reinvigorating a certain client's Honorary Council. It cost them $35,000 and didn't bring in any money. If we had just looked at the direct return and not the process, the council might well have been abandoned. But we knew this work was about the future. One year later, that Honorary Council had spearheaded and supported a $1 million public grant from the state government, an ROI of $28.57 to $1.

Most likely, you will have to discipline yourself to educate your board and senior staff about both sides of the ROI coin to secure a higher return in the future. You will have to show them how fundraising is properly evaluated, or they will continue to pursue it haphazardly.

For this reason, when I served as the CEO of an $8 million California nonprofit, I arranged a regular private lunch with one board member who was overly analytical about the math. It's often necessary to take the time to teach what it takes to get ready for fundraising so that the figure-spouting trustee will be more sympathetic to the process. It worked. He became my biggest advocate for both the process and the math!

What fundraising efforts are *you* working on now, or need to start, that will bear fruit tomorrow if you keep at them? Do these new efforts hold the potential for a very high return, or should you consider a different approach?

Always remember ROI is not just a math exercise. It must include the process steps required to achieve a higher return.

22 Sustainability
Does Not Mean "in Perpetuity"

"I just don't know how to answer that question," he said. The speaker was a director of institutional funding at a cultural organization, one of 110 nonprofit executives attending a leadership summit in Westchester County, New York, at which I was a presenter. He was stumped by a question that had appeared on a grant application. All 109 of his colleagues nodded as he spoke, signifying that in one form or another they too had faced such a question and had trouble finding an answer.

The question? "Can you demonstrate that the program for which you seek funding is sustainable?" My answer was swift: "Sustainability does not mean 'in perpetuity.' A real development plan will do." A dozen people stood in applause, and smiles filled the room.

The National Council of Nonprofits says that the phrase "sustainability" is commonly used to describe a nonprofit that can sustain itself over the long term, perpetuating its ability to fulfill its mission. Sustainability in the nonprofit context includes financial sustainability, as well as leadership succession planning, adaptability, and strategic planning.

This question is, of course, almost laughably ironic, because several years ago, when General Motors, AIG, Lehman Brothers, and other icons of American industry and finance toppled, and the country spiraled into a serious recession, some of the richest private foundations in New York City started to ask nonprofits to demonstrate their sustainability. In other words, they wanted undercapitalized nonprofits to do what corporate giants had failed to do! Yet, it is still a legitimate question, and failing to provide a satisfactory answer may cost you a grant, which is no laughing matter. Whether in a proposal, at a site visit, or in a one-on-one meeting with a donor, you must be prepared to address this question seriously.

Let me suggest three ways for you to think deeply about your answer.

First, there is a certain mythology around the concept of sustainability, which is the root of the anxiety this question triggers. An organization cannot be expected to demonstrate that it is sustainable in perpetuity. It is neither realistic nor appropriate to demand an open-ended projection of program or organizational viability extending into the fuzzy horizons of the indefinite future. If you examine your assumptions about the meaning of sustainability, you will reduce the stress you associate with this concept. You will also realize that the funder could not have shared those assumptions!

General Motors was the global sales leader in cars and trucks for seventy-seven consecutive years. One year before its collapse, Enron was praised for its forward-thinking and projections of growth. AIG, with assets of $800 billion, was the eighteenth largest public company in the world and was held as a model of sustainability. Merrill Lynch, a trillion-dollar colossus, was just six years short of its centennial when it was forced to sell itself to the Bank of America for $50 billion—the same day Lehman Brothers filed for bankruptcy. Executive directors cannot be expected to issue guarantees against an unforeseeable future.

Secondly, if sustainability is not forever, it is, at best, a forecast limited to a finite, manageable period. What is manageable? Generally, three years is about as far ahead as you should reasonably project. The beginning of your answer to the sustainability question should give the funder a precise definition of the period for which you expect the forecast to be valid. If you can only forecast sustainability for eighteen months, then let them know that. You can project a longer time by outlining the conditions required to be successful. For example: "Beyond the eighteen months, we are striving for an additional eighteen months if we have your support for the second and third year and are successful with the challenge gift being presented by our board of directors."

Third, sustainability is not a tangible asset, like a building or a vehicle. It is not something you ever have at a fixed moment. It is intrinsically aspirational. In the absence of a crystal ball, what you can demonstrate to a funder is that your organization has the capacity to approach the objective of sustaining itself across the immediate future. The nonprofit executive who initially raised the subject of sustainability, for instance, represented an organization that was ninety-one years old! Surely, they have done something right to be around that long. I encouraged him to reference its longevity as a reliable indicator that it can sustain its work—past performance is a solid indicator of future success.

Answers to Adapt

With these three considerations in mind, here are examples of sustainability statements that will provide you with many ideas for answering this question based on varied scenarios. Each one indicates an underlying development plan. Of course, I do hope you have a more detailed written development plan, but for our purposes a concise statement showing the heart of your development plan is all we need.

You can customize your own answer based on your unique circumstances, and how much space or time you have to deliver the answer. Here is an example:

We at Community Human Services (CHS) define sustainability as a forecast covering the three years that lie ahead of us. If awarded funding, we are committed to sustaining our programs through this period.

Our capacity to sustain CHS is multi-faceted and based on a neighborhood and programmatic commitment, a diversified development plan, a strategic fundraising plan, and a vibrant organizational culture.

CHS has a programmatic presence in our local community and a network of loyal donors who value the work we are doing. Because of this neighborhood commitment, we are certain that individual giving will continue at a steady pace. We appeal twice a year to our donor base and remain in touch with our donors through the mail, newsletters, and our annual phone bank.

We have a contract with the New York City Department of Education running through 2012 to operate a Get Ahead Program at nearby Bright Prospect High School for 125 at-risk, disconnected youth. However, CHS's approach to development is well thought out, consisting of revenue diversification by introducing new sources of government funds to the agency that are consistent with our program expansion and quality enhancement goals. Our development plan is revisited annually and updated accordingly. We enjoy immediate enhanced capacity to apply for new government funds through our contractual association with LAPA Fundraising. This association allows us to be vigilant about finding new sources of funding and applying for them.

Additionally, in recent years, CHS has greatly increased its private fundraising efforts. We have accelerated our research and proposal submissions to the private and corporate foundation com-

munity. We have also upgraded the sponsorships for our annual events and increased the revenue realized from this source. Through these and other efforts, we are continuing to diversify our funding base and enhance our ability to sustain programs after the period of government support comes to an end.

In the past year, CHS has approached several new grantmakers for support, and we are pleased to report that we have received grants from the A Foundation (for $25,000), the B Foundation ($20,000), the C Foundation ($15,000), and the D Corporation ($10,000). CHS currently has twenty-six grant proposals pending, requesting a total of $625,000.

Working with our board of directors, we have developed and implemented a strategic fundraising plan that will include an expanded annual giving program. Building a larger individual donor base will complement CHS's successful grant-seeking program and help ensure our financial future.

Our past record is a superb indicator of future performance as it demonstrates that this agency is nimble and in touch with current community needs. But we know that at the end of the day, it is the vibrant organizational culture of CHS that sustains our ability to forecast for the future and work toward implementing our dreams for the civil society we seek. At CHS, overall sustainability means that we pay attention to our ongoing cash flow needs, and make sure that we are not dependent upon grants or any other single source of funds. We plan ways to grow our endowment, and we also continue to go deeper within the funding sources that make the most sense for us.

Should you approve our grant request, we will issue a press release and an email alert stating that you have funded us and calling for others to contribute to matching your grant. We will especially let our local legislators know as well and ask them to work with us to submit city council applications for additional years' funding.

How will *you* answer the question about your own organizational sustainability? By examining your assumptions, you will find a path forward. Your answer should capture the heart of your development plan and should focus on what can be reasonably forecasted and managed over the near future. (I prefer a three-year forecast, but others go longer.) Your past performance is a reliable indicator of future success, so be sure to include that where it applies.

Always remember that "sustainability" does not mean "in perpetuity." A real development plan will do.

My dad, a Teamster union member, used to say, "When we stop learning, we die, first inside, then overall." I believe that if we're open to it, our lives can revolve around continually learning, growing, and changing.

For the past twenty-one years, I have spent many weekends on a forty-three-acre wooded homestead in upstate New York with a large lake in the middle, abundant freshwater springs, and twenty-seven species of trees. My visits there have helped me learn about my own change processes, and I have realized that the ecosystem of the forest is based on the principle that nothing goes to waste.

Everything has a purpose, and everything is linked. Plants absorb the energy from the sun and rainwater from the ground, and they produce food, which is eaten by the groundhogs, foxes, turtles, fish, and other creatures. When those animals die, their bodies decompose, becoming a feast for bugs, worms, and microorganisms in the soil and the lakebed, which in turn makes the ground fertile. When plants die, they also decompose, and the seeds they produced give rise to another plant. In the same way, the animals are born, grow, and die, and this entire process begins again and again.

Nothing goes to waste in a forest. The same should be true in your fundraising program.

Your Fundraising Ecosystem

Your fundraising program has its own ecosystem, a revolving cycle of life, death, and rebirth, and you would be wise to be aware of them. Here are a few examples:

Individual Donors = Short Longevity

How long does the average donor give to the same charity? There are many answers to this question, depending on your type of organization. Communications expert Tom Ahern says, "Over half give just once. Very few donors stay longer than a few years: precisely 4.6 years in the UK."[18]

This unfortunate reality means new donor acquisition is essential to your fundraising ecosystem's wellbeing. Yet, so few nonprofits take donor acquisition seriously, let alone take advantage of the latest technology designed to find new value-aligned donor prospects. All donors have a limited life span, and if you're not acquiring new donors, your revenue program will eventually flatline.

Passive Engagement of Major, Major Donors

In Chapter 19, I mentioned the 80/20 rule, which states that roughly 20 percent of your donors will give 80 percent of your revenue. As I have taught for years, however, among that 20 percent, you must give extra special consideration to the top of that group—the 5 percent, who give upwards of 65 percent of your major giving!

---

18 Tom Ahern, "I Asked a Simple Question: How Long Does the Average Donor Stay with a Charity?" May 8, 2016 https://www.aherncomm.com/4933-2/.

Failing to be proactive in stewarding this group and learning about their desire for deeper engagement drives a stake through the heart of your major gift program lifespan. These particular "major, major" donors are the giant sequoia trees of your fundraising forest. They do more for your ecosystem than any other donor because they have the largest capacity to give, assuming they are already in love with your mission and engaged with you.

Short Shelf Life of Private Foundation Giving

There are roughly 105,000 private foundations in the United States. Their revenue typically derives from a single source of funding from which to make grants—usually an individual, family, or business. The foundation invests the majority of its endowment, earning dividends and interest on its investments. The IRS requires private foundations to make grants equal to at least five percent of their investment assets each year and pay a 2 percent excise tax on net investment earnings.

Private foundations are concerned with making a difference in their community, or about a particular issue. They typically have guidelines that will let you know their giving priorities and the focus of their grantmaking. While the guidelines are useful, it is even more instructive to carefully examine a foundation's grants list, which is part of its annual IRS Form 990-PF filing and readily accessible for free at Guidestar.com. By examining the grants list of each foundation, you can get a sense of their giving behavior.

You will also see what I have observed in my twenty-five years of fundraising—that the majority of foundations give for one, two, or three years to a particular nonprofit, and then stop. There are exceptions, but it's generally true, and it means you must be proactive in building new relationships with other institutional funders. To ignore this reality is to put your revenue program at risk.

Building new donor relationships is especially true with the modern phenomena of donor-advised funds because they function like a quasi-private foundation but are not public and do not disclose their giving.

According to the National Philanthropic Trust, in 2017 there were 463,622 individual donor-advised funds across the country. Donors contributed $29.23 billion to these donor-advised funds and used them to recommend $19.08 billion in grants to qualified charities. Both grants and contributions reached record highs. Charitable assets in donor-advised funds totaled $110.01 billion, surpassing the $100 billion mark for the first time.[19]

That being said, this situation only applies to those nonprofits for which private foundation support makes sense. Giving by foundations has seen strong growth for the past seven years (2011-2017), according to data provided by the Foundation Center. The five-year annualized average growth rate of US private foundations was 7.6 percent. This growth far exceeds the 4.3 percent annualized average growth rate for total giving. In real numbers, this was $66.90 billion in private foundation giving for 2017, which is 16 percent of the total $410 billion in total giving that year. I have seen private foundation giving go down as low as 5 percent of the pie. Nonetheless, even when private foundations give, there's a shelf life to their commitment, and you would be wise to analyze the cycles of each foundation that is currently funding you.

Government Contracts that Fall Short of Covering Actual Expenses

Securing a grant contract from your local or state government, or the federal government, is how so many large social service agencies grow. But most contracts do not cover the full costs of operation, and they need to be supplemented with donations from individuals.

There's also the painful issue of slow reimbursement. Government agencies typically do not dole out money in advance; they reimburse you after you spend the money. Waiting for that payment requires the patience of Job and can create a short-term funding gap for your nonprofit. That gap can be covered by a cash

19 The National Philanthropic Trust, the 2018 DAF Report, see https://www.nptrust.org/reports/daf-report/

flow loan from a local foundation or private bank, but that's not always an option.

Further, sometimes these very large contracts create displacement or reduction in other funding. For instance, some individual donors might learn about your grant award, assume that your charity now has enough money, and stop donating. I suggest preventing this problem by explicitly explaining why a private-public partnership is a win-win for all concerned, and "By the way, even with the contract, we need your support to cover the unmet costs!"

Realism

In each one of these examples, you can see the threat at hand, and also the opportunity to optimize—just like the forest's ecosystem—a cycle of life, death, and rebirth. Predictable longevity, passive engagement, shelf lives, and shortfalls are all a part of your fundraising life cycle, but they should not define you. Remember novelist Richard Bach's warning: "Argue for your limitations, and sure enough, they're yours."[20] Instead, let nothing go to waste. Make use of all the ups and downs of your fundraising processes.

The ups and downs can be the basis of incredible learning and show the path for positive change. As nonprofit idealists, we have a moral obligation to envision a better future once our missions succeed. But we must also cherish the challenges we face as opportunities for growth and renewal. I encourage you to let these challenges fuel your creativity.

Admittedly, I am worn down by those whose first response to new ideas is to naysay or explain why it won't work. Frankly, I try to avoid those who only see the cup as half empty; but I am also wary of Pollyanna approaches. Realism replaces these two ends of the spectrum, and fundraising grows best when it's rooted in realistic projections, thoughtful plans, and a sober understanding of which of our fundraising methods are growing, waning, or even

---

20 Richard Bach, *Illusions: The Adventures of a Reluctant Messiah*, (New York: Dell Publishing, 1977), page 12.

dying. Building on a deep awareness that the fundraising ecosystem is continuously changing, it is unlikely your efforts will always achieve the success you desire. It's far more likely that you'll encounter consistent challenges.

James Clear, a self-improvement author, shares tips from proven scientific research. He writes:

> *Evolutionary biologists use a term called 'mismatch conditions' to describe when an organism is not well-suited for a condition it is facing. We have common phrases for mismatch conditions: 'like a fish out of water' or 'bring a knife to a gunfight.' Obviously, when you are in a mismatch condition, it is more difficult to succeed, to be useful, and to win. It is likely you'll face mismatch conditions in your life. At the very least, life will not be optimal—maybe you didn't grow up in the optimal culture for your interests, maybe you were exposed to the wrong subject or sport, maybe you were born at the wrong time in history. It is far more likely that you are living in a mismatch condition than in a well-matched one. Knowing this, you must take it upon yourself to design your ideal lifestyle. You have to turn a mismatch condition into a well-matched one. Optimal lives are designed, not discovered.[21]*

You must take it upon yourself to design your ideal fundraising program. You have to turn a mismatch condition into a well-matched one. Optimal fundraising ecosystems are designed, not discovered, and they must be restored and maintained with tender loving care.

Always remember that in fundraising, nothing goes to waste.

---

21 James Clear, "Entropy: Why Life Always Seems to Get More Complicated." 2018. See https://jamesclear.com/entropy.

At the start, I said this wasn't a "how to" book but a guide to thinking deeply about fundraising. You'll have to judge whether I met that mark.

My ultimate hope is that one or all of these twenty-three big ideas helps your nonprofit advance to the next level of your fundraising program, taking you one step closer to fulfilling your mission and making an impact on the community or cause you serve.

In the introduction, I suggested that these ideas are like popcorn kernels waiting for the heat of your real dilemmas to pop them open and make them relevant. Once the pop of awareness occurs, these chapters can help you make good choices about how to resolve and move beyond your particular dilemma.

I have no doubt that you will find your way, just as I have.

As you know well by now, Peter F. Drucker helped me find my way. I can see him in my mind's eye leaning forward in his chair and peering down from the elevated stage, saying, "Your most important task is to anticipate crisis, and have a plan for how to deal with it." In *Managing The Nonprofit Organization*, Peter explained, "Leadership Is a Foul-Weather Job," he explained, "The most important task of an organization's leader is to anticipate crisis. Perhaps not to avert it, but to anticipate it. To wait until the crisis hits is already abdication. One has to make the organization capable of anticipating the storm, weathering it, and in fact, being ahead of it. That is called innovation, constant renewal." (p.9)

Do you now feel more prepared to avert crisis in your fundraising program? I surely hope that you do.

If you do, think of Benjamin Franklin's invitation, "He that has once done you a kindness will be more ready to do you another, than whom you yourself have obliged." This axiom is called the "Ben Franklin effect"—when someone helps you once, they want to help you again because it feels good.

I feel confident about what I have shared in these pages, and should you find these lessons valuable to your work, I hope you will be kind enough to pass on your thoughts to colleague.

I very much welcome your comments, questions, and reflections at https://laurencepagnoni.org.

Bibliography

Ahern, T. (2016). "I Asked a Simple Question: How Long Does the Average Donor Stay with a Charity?" Retrieved from http://www.aherncomm.com/4933-2.

Bach, R. (1977). *Illusions: The Adventures of a Reluctant Messiah*. New York, NY: Dell Publishing.

Bekkers, R., and Wiepking, P. (2010). "A Literature Review of Empirical Studies of Philanthropy: Eight Mechanisms That Drive Charitable Giving." *Nonprofit and Voluntary Sector Quarterly 40*(5), 924-973.

"Building a Stewardship Matrix" [PDF file]. (n.d.). Retrieved from https://www.trec.org/wp-content/uploads/2015/02/Stewarship-Matrix_v818.pdf.

Bur, M. (2017). "Why the High Employee-Turnover Rate?" Retrieved from https://www.nonprofitpro.com/article/43895.

Clear, J. (2018). "Entropy: Why Life Always Seems to Get More Complicated." Retrieved from https://jamesclear.com/entropy

Collins, J. (2001). *Good to Great: Why Some Companies Make the Leap...And Others Don't.* New York, NY: Harper Collins.

Collins, J., and Porras, J. (2002). *Built to Last: Successful Habits of Visionary Companies.* New York, NY: Harper Collins.

Dreyfus, S.N. (2018). "Volunteerism and US Civil Society." *Stanford Social Innovation Review*. Retrieved from https://ssir.org/articles/entry/volunteerism_and_us_civil_society.

Drucker, P. (1990). *Managing the Non-profit Organization: Principles and Practices.* New York, NY: Harper Collins.

"Engaging Nonprofit Employees: Industry Report." (n.d.). Retrieved from https://www.quantumworkplace.com/engaging-nonprofit-employees.

Foster, W. and Fine, G. (2007). "How Nonprofits Get Really Big." *Stanford Social Innovation Review, 5*(2), 46-55.

Greenfield, J. (1999). *Fund Raising: Evaluating and Managing the Fund Development Process.* New York, NY: John Wiley and Sons.

Infographic: Why Nonprofit Employees Quit. (n.d.). Retrieved from https://blog.techimpact.org/infographic-why-nonprofits-employees-quit.

Kidder, T. (2004). *Mountains Beyond Mountains: The Quest of Dr. Paul Farmer, a Man Who Would Cure the World.* New York, NY: Random House.

Konrath, S., and Handy, F. (2017). "5 Reasons why people give their money away—plus 1 why they don't." *The Conversation.* Retrieved from https://theconversation.com/5-reasons-why-people-give-their-money-away-plus-1-why-they-dont-87801.

Mathiasen, K. (1990). "Board Passages: Three Stages in a Nonprofit Board's Lifecycle" [PDF file]. Retrieved from https://boardsource.org/three-stages-nonprofit-board-lifecycle.

"Measuring Fundraising Effectiveness—It's Time to Get it Right." (2017). Retrieved from https://trust.guidestar.org/measuring-fundraising-effectiveness-its-time-to-get-it-right.

Nayar, V. (2010). *Employees First, Customers Second: Turning Conventional Management Upside Down.* Boston, MA: Harvard Business School Publishing.

Nonprofit Finance Study. (2018). Retrieved from https://www.abila.com/resource-library/research-report/nonprofit-finance-study-dynamics-challenges-growth.

Nouwen, H. (2010). *The Spirituality of Fundraising*. Nashville, TN: Upper Room Books.

"Overview of Overall Giving." (2017). The Indiana University Lilly Family School of Philanthropy. Retrieved from http://generosityforlife.org/wp-content/uploads/2017/10/Overall-Giving-10.5.17-jb-CJC.pdf.

Pagnoni, L., and Solomon, M. (2013). *The Nonprofit Fundraising Solution: Powerful Revenue Strategies to Take You to the Next Level*. New York, NY: AMACOM.

Pallotta, D. (2010). *Uncharitable*. Lebanon, NH: University Press of New England.

"Peter Drucker." (2000, January 1). *The Wall Street Journal*. Retrieved from https://www.wsj.com/articles/SB113208136049697833.

Philanthropy Panel Study. (n.d.). Retrieved from https://philanthropy.iupui.edu/research/current-research/philanthropy-panel-study.html.

Rosen, M. (2011). *Donor-Centered Planned Gift Marketing*. Hoboken: John Wiley & Sons.

Rosen, M. (2018). Do You Really Have What It Takes to be a Successful Fundraising Professional? Retrieved from https://michaelrosensays.wordpress.com/2018/04/08/do-you-really-have-what-it-takes-to-be-a-successful-fundraising-professional.

Segedin, A. (2016). Finance And Fundraising Equals Water And Oil. *The Nonprofit Times*. Retrieved from https://www.thenonprofittimes.com/npt_articles/finance-and-fundraising-equals-water-and-oil.

Slaper, T., and Hall, T. (2011). "The Triple Bottom Line: What Is It and How Does It Work?" *Indiana Business Review 86*(1). Retrieved from http://www.ibrc.indiana.edu/ibr/2011/spring/article2.html.

The 2018 DAF Report. (2018). Retrieved from https://www.nptrust.org/reports/daf-report.

"The Sorry State of Nonprofit Boards." (2015). *Harvard Business Review*. Retrieved from https://hbr.org/2015/09/the-sorry-state-of-nonprofit-boards.

"Understanding and Evaluating Your Fundraising Strategy: A Toolkit and Conversation Guide for Boards and Leadership Teams." (n.d.). Retrieved from https://www.theboarddoctor.info/uploads/7/8/3/9/78398336/79._measuring_fundraising_effectiveness_toolkit.pdf.

Index

If you liked this book, you'll also want to read...

Real-world solutions to take any fundraising program from good to great.

Powerful Revenue Strategies to Take You to the Next Level

THE NONPROFIT FUNDRAISING SOLUTION

LAURENCE A. PAGNONI
with Michael Solomon

About the Author

LAURENCE A. PAGNONI has spent 25 years in the nonprofit sector as a fundraising consultant and the executive director of three nonprofit organizations. He is chairman of LAPA Fundraising and the author of *INFO*, a popular blog about cutting-edge nonprofit fundraising. A long-standing member of the Association of Fundraising Professionals (AFP), Laurence has served on the AFP Planning Committee for Fundraising Day in New York City and teaches workshops on fundraising and management topics.

Visit his website at: www.thenonprofitfundraisingsolution.com

Email Laurence directly at: lpagnoni@lapafundraising.com

ISBN: 978-0-8144-3296-9
Paperback, $19.95

Your nonprofit needs revenue to fulfill its mission. In the face of government cutbacks, shrinking endowments, and business belt-tightening, securing funds can be a daunting challenge. But armed with the right strategies, you can take your organization far beyond mere survival to thrive in any economic environment.

Presenting real-life stories and "casebooks" of strategies in action, *The Nonprofit Fundraising Solution* bridges the gap between theory and practical methods and shows you how to:

• Determine the right level of funding diversification

• Build a broad constituency of donors aligned to your mission

• Ensure that executive leadership and board dynamics fully support your fundraising initiatives

• Proactively encourage planned giving

• Avoid revenue plateaus

Revealing the inextricable link between successful fundraising and organizational development, the book shows how to increase your access to wealthy donors and raise your community profile to power revenue through tactics such as challenge drives, stretch gifts, and corporate matching gifts; parlor gatherings; leadership councils; year-end drives; corporate partnerships; and major campaigns.

To survive and ultimately thrive, your organization needs forceful revenue strategies and an organizational culture that champions them. This book demonstrates how to implement advanced fundraising methods to secure the funds you need to excel.

AMACOM
THE BOOK PUBLISHING DIVISION OF
AMERICAN MANAGEMENT ASSOCIATION

Single copies available at your favorite online retailer or bookstore.
Great discounts on bulk purchases, starting at 40%!
For details, call 1-800-250-5308 or email: SpecSlsWeb@amanet.org

Made in the USA
Columbia, SC
10 July 2020